TACTICAL
PISTOL SHOOTING

2nd Edition

Erik Lawrence
& Mike Pannone

Published by

Gun Digest® Books, an imprint of F+W Media, Inc.
Krause Publications • 700 East State Street • Iola, WI 54990-0001
715-445-2214 • 888-457-2873
www.krausebooks.com

To order books or other products call toll-free 1-800-258-0929
or visit us online at www.krausebooks.com, www.gundigeststore.com
or www.Shop.Collect.com

Library of Congress Control Number: 2009925862

ISBN-13: 978-1-4402-0436-4
ISBN-10: 4402-0436-5

Cover Design by Tom Nelsen
Designed by Elizabeth Krogwold
Edited by Corrina Peterson

Printed in China

DEDICATION

This book is dedicated to the Soldiers, Marines, and Airmen fighting in the Global War on Terrorism, defending our freedoms and lifestyle.

Train more! Fight less!

ACKNOWLEDGMENTS

I would like to thank the following individuals for making this revision as smooth and painless as possible, yet bringing it up to where tactical pistol shooting is at the present time:

Mike Pannone, for assisting with translating the different viewpoints on this subject and adding to this book to make it more well-rounded and relevant to today's operators. Mike's points on common-sense safety and body mechanics are without equal. "Don't fake the funk as you will get caught sooner or later!"

The late Colonel Jeff Cooper, who allowed me the privilege of using many of his points to explain best the needed mindset for tactical operations, which is the basis for Chapter One.

Jason "Sapper" Larimore, for being the IT and photography guru who is instrumental to all our book projects.

Karen Poppele, for once again turning my scratching into English so others may somehow understand what I am attempting to explain.

Krause Publishing, for carrying this book and agreeing to allow this much-needed revision to bring the ideas up to speed.

ABOUT THE AUTHOR

Erik Lawrence has served with the U.S. Army Special Forces and/or U.S. Government for the last 20 years. During this time, he has trained, deployed and operated in many conflicts, allowing him to perfect his instructor skills with real-world examples that allow for perspective in the need for proper training. Having trained and advised numerous U. S. Military and foreign military units in specialized tactical training, Erik has perfected his ability to deliver relevant and correct training for up-coming generations of law enforcement and warfighters. As the Man-aging Member of Blackheart International, LLC, he created Mid-Atlantic Training Resources, LLC, to provide much-needed proper and thorough tactical training.

Mastering the basics is the only way to shoot faster or more accu-rately, and this goal can be achieved only with proper instruction and critiques. This consolidated, easy-to-read handbook provides a base knowledge that offers laymen and/or professional operators the refer-ences to learn/maintain their skills with their pistol, thus raising their level of safety and competence. Whether you carry a pistol for a living or for defense, this book will help you attain the level of training desired.

- Managing Member of Mid-Atlantic Training Resources, LLC
- National Rifle Association Law Enforcement Firearms Instructor
- West Virginia Law Enforcement Governor's Board Instructor
- Federal Law Enforcement Training Instructor for Federal Air Marshal program
- Numerous military instructor and shooting/tactics courses
- Instructor of multiple courses, from pistol to foreign weapons armorer courses
- Author of multiple firearms manuals and tactics publications

CONTENTS

INTRODUCTION

Think of how many "professionals" carry a firearm, yet only once in their life are they trained to use it, followed by years of qualifications. After seeing this occurrence time after time, I began to write this book to assist self-motivated individuals (professional gun carriers or Jo Civilian concealed-weapon carriers) to better their foundation in safe and effective handgun skills/usage.

As this handbook is a revision of the original work, I have asked for input from many personal sources to update techniques more effectively and look for better ways to explain procedures for ease in learning.

This book's objective is to share the knowledge of pistolcraft that Mike Pannone and I have gained over the years while serving together in the U.S. Army Special Forces and doing what we have both done since then. My name is Erik Lawrence, and both Mike and I each have 20 years in Special Forces/real-world experience. While in Special Forces, we trained, consulted, and operated in many countries with some of the host countries' most elite police and military units. Since leaving the military, we have continued to travel, operate, and provide weapons training to a host of foreign countries under U.S. Government contract for these services. We will caution you that the shooting community is full of armchair experts – those with diplomas and no experience, and the "I could tell you but I would have to kill you" types. Also remember not all good shooters can teach you to shoot; you need good instructors who know how to use adult-learning techniques to relay the skills needed to perform properly.

Skill with the pistol is the measure of shooting proficiency in many units around the globe. While you can be a lousy pistol shot and still be a good rifle shot, your best sniper is an expert with a pistol. You cannot hide with a pistol at pistol-shooting distances; you can either shoot well or not. Through the years, we have continually discovered it is the mastering of the basics that allows a shooter to progress to an "advanced" level, which means doing the basics faster and more accurately.

We have also arrived at many conclusions on handgun and accessories selection based on quality of manufacture and simplicity. Many of these will be covered in this book with explanations of our opinions. But no expensive handgun or accessory will replace true skill and solid fundamentals in a less-than-desirable situation.

It cannot be over-emphasized that the difference between marksmanship and combat marksmanship is truly the difference between practicing against paper and fighting for your life. We have encountered many examples of this since the original printing of this book, as we have been quite busy with the multiple theaters of war in which we have participated. We have reaffirmed that some fundamental rules must be bent to conduct effective combat marksmanship, but with the proper training and foundation, they may be performed safely, ef-

> *"Receive good, sound instruction and practice, practice, and practice some more."*

fectively, and quickly. This book details the use of the pistol in the development of your skills to improve combat marksmanship, not bulls-eye shooting.

I will restate that the most important points I can bring out are to receive good, sound instruction and practice, practice, and practice some more. I don't mean you should go out to the range for 12 hours and fire thousands of rounds; you should train efficiently and be organized – like going to the gym. Have a plan of why you are going and know what drills you will practice and then how to execute the exercise while perfecting the proper form/fundamentals. Make sure you have a checklist of what you need for this practice rather than finding out after you are at the range that you are missing needed gear, possibly causing a mental breakdown since no one has enough time for practice. This version of the book will have more logbook pages in the appendix to encourage you track your progress and maintain a proper training record.

This revised edition is not meant to be the all-inclusive bible for handgunners; it is simply another source of information from which to learn and further your personal progress as a shooter or instructor. Take this book as another tool for your toolbox, and never say, "I know enough."

Comments may be directed to my contact information in the back of the book, but do not waste your time sending argumentative comments. Constructive criticism is welcomed to allow for my learning to progress also.

This book was written with the right-handed individual shooting a modern semiautomatic pistol in mind. Some techniques may transfer to the use of the revolver but should be analyzed first. Left-handed shooters should read Chapter 12 of this book for its specific techniques, as well as seek professional instruction.

Do not take this book lightly when it details the dirty truth about neutralizing targets. Targets are human beings, so you must accept this point before you seriously take on combat-oriented pistol shooting. Competitions are fun and organized; spur-of-the-moment close gunfights are neither fun nor organized. The most important thing to have in your possession at that time is the training in your head and how to apply it to the situation at hand. "Train as you fight" should be your motivation to attain your acceptable standard.

CHAPTER ONE

MINDSET

The use of a pistol for life-or-death encounters should be taken very seriously. Not much else is more important than saving your life and possibly taking someone else's. You must realize this early on. Think about it. Make peace with your idea of right and wrong. Studies have shown that some people, when involved in kill-or-be-killed situations, allowed themselves to be killed rather than take the life of another. This choice is obviously a personal one, but you must prepare yourself mentally for the decision. I also feel it would be much better to avoid such situations through the use of individual and family protective measures, which I have detailed in my 2007 revision of *Everyday Protection for Everyday People, 2nd edition* - ISBN 978-0-9800678-0-4.

The first edition of this book overlooked the fact that Col. Jeff Cooper of Gunsite, Inc., provided this first chapter. Many thanks to him and his organization for this assistance. Col. Cooper recently passed away, but his points remain valid for today and in the future. This chapter is based on Cooper's 1989 book, *Principles of Personal Defense*. His study of this subject continues to be the measuring device for its presentation and development. A discussion of the combat mindset is paramount to using a pistol effectively and is thus presented before we get into the mechanics of shooting.

What is "MENTAL CONDITIONING"?

Decent human beings have difficulty with the thought of needlessly injuring or killing another human being. We have been raised to embrace the standards of fairness, equality, kindness, gentleness and goodness toward others. Unfortunately, there are many others in the world today who have no value or sense of goodness towards others.

Contrary to the exhortations of the elite, there are wolves out there – the two-legged type – and you will run across them. These individuals do not abide by laws of our government or the social standards of ethical conduct. They consider armed robbery their personal right, and your money their pay. Others in the world today believe that the religion they practice demands the exclusion of all others and even the lives of any "unbelievers." And of course still others, who are truly and clinically emotionally disturbed, possess no sense of right or wrong. Whatever the reason, many would kill or injure you, or your family, or your friends, without remorse.

Another social reality is that the police of our society cannot protect us. Law enforcement is under no occupational obligation to do so. In fact, their job is defined as a *post-event* response. Investigations and the court system are a post-event system. Department of Justice and FBI statistics estimate that one in every four adults in America will be a part of, victim of, or witness to a violent crime over the next 10 years. Interpersonal conflict is a fact

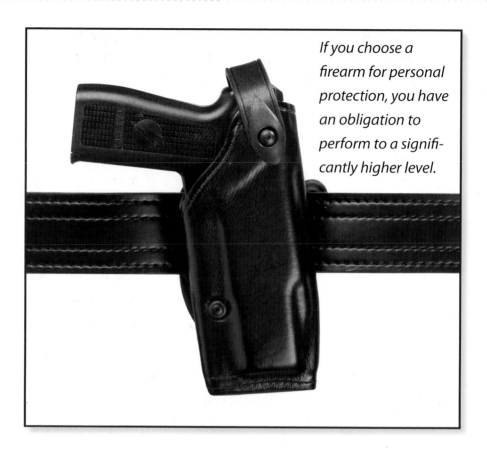

If you choose a firearm for personal protection, you have an obligation to perform to a significantly higher level.

of life. It is in response to this issue that many people are deciding to increase their ability for self-protection. The number of states offering some type of concealed-carry permits for citizens has grown to 48, and two states, Alaska and Vermont, allow carry with no permit at all for non-felons. As of July 2008, two states (Wisconsin and Illinois) and Washington, D.C. have no provision for legal concealed carry.

Personal protection is not a new concept. This is the logical reason that many American citizens, starting from the Constitutional forefathers, have chosen to keep a firearm for self-defense. Whatever your method or plan of personal protection, you should take the responsibility to defend yourself and your family. The character trait of pro-active personal defense is not paranoia, nor is it fatalism. It provides the ability to answer more questions about life and living with increased peace of mind.

Bear in mind that if you choose to increase your ability in the area of personal defense you must not initiate an attack. That is unlawful and immoral. However, action is always faster than reaction. If someone initiates an attack, you will have to play catch-up. The only way to increase the chances of survival is through pre-conditioning or mental conditioning. This pre-conditioning of our minds permits us to defend ourselves more easily and survive an interpersonal crisis or deadly encounter.

If you choose a firearm for personal protection, you have an obligation to perform to a significantly higher level. Carrying any weapon brings with it a higher legal, moral and ethical standard. The armed citizen must be cognizant of his surroundings; he must be able to anticipate and avoid, if possible, any potentially dangerous situations. If an armed citizen is unable to avoid a lethal confrontation, he must be able to devote his entire being to resolving the situation at hand. And he must possess the self-control necessary to know when and how to use, or how not to use, Deadly Physical Force.

Combat Triad

The Combat Triad is the foundation of the doctrine taught to help students identify, assess and respond to potential life-threatening decisions. It is composed of three elements: gunhandling, marksmanship and mindset (mental conditioning). They may be briefly defined as follows:

Gunhandling: The ability to manipulate safely and responsibly the weapon/firearm. It entails presentation (deploying), loading, reloading, unloading, reducing malfunctions and ready (responsive) positions.

Marksmanship: The ability to align firearm sights while controlling the trigger without disturbing the sight alignment.

Mindset: Your mind is what will keep you alive in a gunfight. Your mind is your real weapon. Thus, the proper mindset is paramount. The type of weapon, the caliber or the holster in which you carry your firearm is not as important as your state of mind.

For example, gunhandling and marksmanship will allow a student to get a handgun into operation quickly for a rapid response to a threat. Anyone possessing average coordination can draw and hit a target at seven yards in 1.5 seconds. But…can you do it when your life is at stake and *under fire*? As you can see, the combat mindset is imperative.

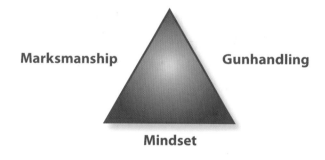

Marksmanship   Gunhandling

Mindset

Combat Mindset

What really is the mindset? It is a state of mind that ensures survival in a gunfight or in a life-threatening crisis. The backbone of the combat mindset is the essence of self-control. Certainly there is some overlap with the elements of the combat triad since dexterity and marksmanship are a prerequisite to confidence, and confidence is a prerequisite to self-control. However, for the self-control used in the combat mindset, awareness, anticipation and concentration are required.

To assist individuals in developing the awareness needed in a personal security doctrine, Col. Jeff Cooper, USMC (Ret.), modified the military alert code for civilian use. This Color Code of Awareness originated at Gunsite and is probably the single-most effective method that one can use to avoid, or counter, a life-threatening situation. Four colors keep it simple. There is no reason to add others. The colors make it easy to visualize and remember. They have nothing to do with whether or not you are armed. The Color Code helps to pre-condition your mind for the possibility of a violent attack.

Again, we do not initiate an attack. Someone else will, and we will have to play catch up. Pre-conditioning permits us to defend ourselves more easily and survive that deadly encounter.

Color Code Of Awareness

White: The color white can be considered to be the absence of alertness. A person in White is totally relaxed, completely unprepared and absolutely unaware of his surroundings. Pilots call this condition, "Fat, Dumb and Happy." It is too large a mental jump to get into a combat or reactive mode from White. Possibly the only time you are at White is inside your own home as you may have a security system, dogs and weapons in and around the home which allow for delayed and planned responses. If you are attacked while in White, regardless of your ability or equipment, you may not survive.

Yellow: Yellow is the state of mind in which one is relaxed with a non-specific alert. There is no immediate threat, but you are alert to any possibility. In Yellow you may not be approached unaware. This increased awareness from White increases your ability to shift into a reactive or combat mode. You are not looking for trouble, but are prepared if it happens. A good example of Yellow is when you are operating your automobile. You are constantly scanning your mirrors, constantly looking for someone to do something that may cause a problem for you. Your seat belt is on, although you are not anticipating a collision. Yellow is comfortable and you can stay in it indefinitely.

Orange: Orange represents a specific alert. Someone, something or some action has attracted your attention. A crisis or violent assault may be indicated. There may be a harmless explanation for this, but you must have an answer before standing down to Yellow. It is much easier to move into your reactive or fighting mode from the awareness state of Orange than from Yellow.

Red: Red is the knowledge that "The fight is on." This is the state of mind when your "mental trigger" or "go button" is tripped. The mental trigger may be a firearm pointed at you, a man rapidly approaching you with an upraised bat or advancing toward you with a knife, or any other gesture that you have pre-determined to be potentially life-threatening. The mental trigger may depend on a variety of circumstances, but the decision to use deadly physical force has been made. It may not result in your having to use this force, but the decision has already been made by you. If they do "that," you will do "this." From Red, you will not have to play "catch-up" mentally. You are ready.

With the color code, you do not have to move up (or down) the list sequentially. You can jump from Yellow to Red, bypassing Orange. But, White has been shown to have too long a dwell time for response to critical situations. Once you begin practicing and increasing your awareness with the color code, other elements of mental conditioning will help you determine how your reaction should be employed for crisis intervention. These elements are called the principles of self-defense.

Principles of Self Defense

Alertness

- Be aware of all that is around you.

- Know what is behind you (remember 360° security).

- Pay particular attention to anything that is out of place. (What's wrong with this picture?)

- Trust your instinct. Your stomach has no ego. If it is queasy, there is probably a reason for it.

- Set your mental condition to Yellow. Don't get caught in White.

Decisiveness

- Select a correct course of action and carry it through without hesitation or deviation.

- He who hesitates is indeed lost.

Aggressiveness

- We do not initiate, but thereafter should return the attention with what should be overwhelming violence.

"A simple plan, well rehearsed and violently executed, offers the best chance for success."

-- *RANGER HANDBOOK*
AS PER RANGER WILBURN

- Your response if attacked should not be fear, but anger. Fear can be changed into anger. Do it. They should NOT have the right to do that! They will not have the right!

Speed

- Speed is the key absolute in any form of effective combat.
- The perfect fight is over before the loser really understands what is going on.

Coolness (and if firearms are used, Precision)

- Controlled anger is no obstacle to efficiency.
- If you know that you can keep your head, and know that you must keep your head, you probably will keep your head.

Ruthlessness

- The attack must be stopped. *Do not hold back*.
- Your first concern is to stay alive.

> *"I may lose a battle, but I will never lose a minute."*
>
> -NAPOLEON

> *"Never, never, never give up."*
>
> - WINSTON CHURCHILL

- Strike no more after he is incapable of action, but see that he is stopped!

Surprise

- Surprise is the first principle of offensive combat.

- Do what your assailant least expects you to do.

- Achieve tactical surprise. The criminal does not expect you to fight back. May he never choose you, but if he does, surprise *him*.

Probably the most common question about the principles of personal defense relates to fear. Fear is one of man's greatest motivators. How do we examine fear and make it work for us?

You can encounter many situations where a white visible light source—a flashlight—can greatly increase your chance of survival.

Fear

Fear is said to have three components. They are:

- Cognitive: Which is an anticipatory anxiety—a sixth sense.

- Physiological: From our body's chemical cocktail of adrenaline.

- Overt behavior: The manifestation of our actions.

  Learn that fear takes time to build. It is physiologically and psychologically similar to anger. Anger is the proper antidote to fear. How? Gain the knowledge of your mind and body's stress responses. Recognize them and learn what you can do to direct those physiological actions.

PSYCHOLOGISTS CALL THIS A "STARTLE RESPONSE":

- If caught unaware, the head will crunch down into shoulders. Some may "freeze." You can train out of this.

- Chemical Cocktail- Adrenaline, cortisol and dopamine are released into your system. These cause blood to be diverted from skin, extremities and digestive organs to the large muscle groups related to speed and strength. (This is the "fight or flight" response.)

- Nausea is caused as a portion of the blood supply from the stomach is shifted to large muscle groups.

- The heart/lungs work harder and faster. The rhythm and volume are increased. Tachycardia- The heart rate doubles. Breathing increases.

- The blood pressure increases in response to the heart and adrenaline (another reason to stay in shape).

- Spleen discharges additional red blood cells to increase the oxygen supply.

- Sweat glands kick in to increase body cooling.

- General muscle groups tighten, limiting mobility.

- Extra blood is made available for large muscle groups, providing less blood for small muscle groups, resulting in less dexterity. (This point is why we emphasize gross motor skills.)

- Saliva glands shut down. Dry mouth occurs.

- Auditory exclusion- Both physical and physiological. Gunshots and other sounds may not be clearly heard.

- Tunnel vision- Eyes dilate. Focus may be on opponent's weapon, but other objects blur.

- Visual slowdown- Things may appear to be happening in slow motion.

- Time- Spatial distortion.

- Denial- "Is this really happening to me?" Some may be stuck here. If this is the case, you will lose.

- Altered decision process.

*Watch your front sight
and control the trigger
straight to the rear.*

Survival Stress Management

You can manage the effects of fear and the startle response through survival stress management:

- Immediately slow your breathing (tactical breathing).
- Prioritize the threats. (How do we eat an elephant? One plate at a time.)
- Visualize what needs to be done to stop the attack.
- Take the proper course of action.

Studies indicate that certain types of individuals may be pre-disposed to survive life-threatening situations. These types include, but are not limited to:

- Those with aggressive personalities.

- Pre-conditioned individuals.

- Those who have survived similar situations in the past.

   In order to survive, you must first accept that this can, and may, happen to you. You must be prepared to deal with this type of situation at any time. You cannot make an appointment for an emergency; you must deal with it NOW!

- Meet the threat. Accept that it is there. This can happen to me!

- Everything fits into the operational concept. Fit it in yours.

- Develop a street-smart mindset.

- Your attitude should be composed of self-control and concentration.

- The excitement won't kill you, but surprise will.

- Don't get locked into stereotypes. The threat may be male or female, young or old, Black, White, Hispanic, Asian, or whatever. Be alert.

- Above all, you must have the confidence and ability to win. The Combat Triad. Watch your front sight and control the trigger straight to the rear.

   When combined, the aspects of the color code and the principles of defense, pistolcraft, mental awareness and mindset provide the groundwork necessary to develop a personal security doctrine.

In a life-threatening situation, you will default to your level of training.

The Personal Security Doctrine

A personal security doctrine is key to establishing effective pro-active personal protection. The "Keys" to Threat Avoidance are:

- A street-smart mindset.

- Threat analysis.

- Tradecraft.

Street-smart Mindset

MENTAL PREPARATION:

- Defeatism will defeat…YOU!

- Even if you are forced to give up, don't give in.

- Accept responsibility for your actions. What you do in a heartbeat will be reviewed by many others over a long period of time. Deal with it.

- Don't be a victim. Don't look like prey.

MENTAL CONDITIONING:

- Your mind is like your body. It must be conditioned to respond.

- You have to build on your training. The skills are perishable and the training must be continuous. Stay current!

- In a life-threatening situation, you will not rise to the occasion; you will simply default to your level of training.

MENTAL AWARENESS:

- Color codes

- Simulations…Practice the "What if?"

Threat Analysis

Situational awareness: What is the nature of the threat? Home invasion, street robbery, car jacking, larceny from or of auto, etc.

- Time of day: Violent crimes are more likely to occur after dark

- Public events or significant social anniversaries

- Geography: High-crime neighborhoods, locations, and places

Tradecraft

Training with self-defense tools (standard/improvised), distance and movement. Distance is your friend. Get the best and most training you can.

- Alter routes to bypass hazardous areas

- Surveillance detection

- All aspects of threat avoidance are intertwined

- Avoid dangerous situations, every time you can

If you cannot avoid danger, do whatever you must to stay alive.

Be Prepared – Not Paranoid

Once trained, visually rehearse different situations. Many training courses use this visualization to allow for practice wherever you are. This allows you to be quicker at deciding what course of action you are going to execute. It is free, no one can stop you from doing it at any time, and you decide what the situation will be. Once trained, you will be able to make timely, intelligent decisions to solve problems.

CHAPTER TWO

PISTOL NOMENCLATURE & TERMS

+P: Ammunition that is loaded to higher pressures than standard ammunition. Typical examples include 9mm+P and .38 Special +P.

+P+: Ammunition loaded to even higher pressures than +P ammunition.

Action: The series of moving parts that allow a pistol to be loaded, fired and unloaded.

Autoloader: A pistol that automatically reloads itself as long as it has rounds in its magazine.

Backstrap: Rear vertical portion of the pistol frame between the grip panels.

Barrel: The metal tube through which a projectile passes on its way to the target; contains the riflings that produce the spin for stable flight of the bullet.

Bore: The inside of the barrel.

Break of the shot: The instant the weapon fires.

Caliber: Diameter of the bullet and the distance between the lands and grooves of the bore.

Cartridge: Ammunition completely assembled with the projectile, powder, case and primer.

Centerfire: Cartridge with the primer centered in the base of the case.

Chamber: The rear part of a barrel in which a cartridge is contained when it is loaded and fired.

Clip: Metal device that holds loaded rounds and assists loading into a magazine; most call magazines "clips," but they are quite different in their appearance and their uses.

Concealment: Anything that hides you from view, but does not provide enough protection to stop bullets.

Controlled pair: Two well-aimed shots that have three distinct sight pictures (one before the first shot and one after each shot); the second shot should be delivered as soon as the pistol has settled enough to reacquire the correct sight picture and sight alignment. Used when the distance or size of the target requires a very accurate shot.

Cover: A barrier that will stop bullets and thus protect you from being shot.

Cross-eye dominant: When a shooter's dominant side is different than his dominant eye. Example: a right-handed person who is left-eye dominant.

Cycle of operation: The functions of the pistol during firing. This cycle is firing, unlocking, extracting, ejecting, cocking, feeding, chambering and locking.

Decocking lever: The mechanical part of the pistol that allows the shooter to lower the hammer safely on a cocked pistol. Most double-action pistols are built with one for safety.

Discriminating fire: Shooting engagements that are conducted with both good and hostile targets in the same area. Shots must be taken only at the hostile targets, with no collateral damage to the friendly targets.

Double action: A pistol that both cocks and releases the hammer or internal firing mechanism when the trigger is pulled.

Double-feed malfunction: See failure-to-extract malfunction.

Double tap: A type of engagement that places two rapidly fired shots consecutively onto a single target. Flash sight pictures are acquired to speed up the engagement. The distance and size of the target greatly determine whether you use a controlled pair or a double tap-type engagement.

Dry firing: The act of practicing with your equipment and pistol without using ammunition. You can use dummy weapons, ammunition and/or magazines.

Ejector: The pistol part that ejects the empty casing or cartridge from the pistol.

Failure-to-fire malfunction: This malfunction is created by the operator's attempt to fire on an empty chamber or a defective round, which will not fire. Refer to Chapter Eight - Malfunction Drills.

Failure-to-extract malfunction: This malfunction (sometimes called the "double feed") is created when the fired casing in the chamber is not extracted from the chamber and the next round is rammed behind it in the pistol's attempt to feed the next round. Refer to Chapter Eight - Malfunction Drills.

Failure-to-eject malfunction: This malfunction (sometimes called the "stovepipe") is created when the spent casing is not fully ejected from the weapon during firing. Typically they are vertical or horizontal stovepipe malfunctions that are created when the casing is caught by the return of the slide to chamber the next round. Chapter Eight - Malfunction Drills.

Firing foot: The strong-side foot. For the right-handed shooter, it is the right foot and opposite for the left-handed shooter.

Firing pin: The mechanical part of the pistol that strikes the primer on the round when the hammer is released.

Flash sight picture: Using the front sight only to engage targets quickly. You may also superimpose the rear profile of the pistol onto the target to speed up the engagement. This technique must be practiced as it is less accurate if not conducted correctly. The distance and size of the target greatly influence the use of a flash sight picture.

Frame: The main part of the pistol that is the building block on which all other parts are attached.

Front strap: The front of the pistol's grip that is below the trigger guard.

Grip: The handle part of the pistol you grasp; also the term for the way you hold the pistol with your hands.

Hammers: The firing of two very rapid shots with only one sight picture; your target is large and is close enough to hit during recoil from the first round.

Hangfire: A noticeable delay in the ignition of a cartridge after the primer has been struck by the firing pin.

High-ready position: A resting position with a two-handed grip on the pistol and the muzzle oriented 45 degrees into the air. This position is unsafe in my view and is not taught. When this is practiced on the range and then applied to tactical operations, it makes the chance of an accidental discharge into someone's head too likely (close proximity to team members and high stress can equal an avoidable disaster). It is now popular to call step three of the draw and presentation the high ready; this is semantics.

Kneeling position: This shooting position is used when you need to utilize low cover or a lower, steadier position from which to shoot—very useful when shooting while wounded. Refer to Chapter Six - Shooting Positions.

Low-ready position: A shooting position that is utilized to rest in between drills or while waiting for a situation to change. Chapter Six - Shooting Positions.

Magazine: A storage device designed to hold rounds ready for insertion into the chamber.

Magazine release: The mechanical device that allows you to remove the magazine that is locked in the magazine well. On pistols, this is usually a button.

Magazine spring: The spring in the magazine that forces the loaded rounds to the top of the magazine.

Malfunction: Anytime a weapon fails to operate. There are three types of malfunctions that we will deal with: failure-to-fire, stovepipe and double feed. Refer to Chapter Eight - Malfunction Drills.

Misfire: A cartridge that failed to fire when the primer was struck by the firing pin.

Mozambique drills: This drill is a type of failure-to-stop drill. When the target is not neutralized by normal target engagement techniques, this method is used to ensure neutralization. At least two shots are fired to the center of mass (the chest); then at least one round is fired at the upper center of mass (the head).

Muzzle: The front end of the barrel from which the bullet exits.

Muzzle flash: The amount of flash produced when you fire your pistol. The barrel length, type of powder and powder charge, along with the atmospheric conditions and ambient light level, determine the brightness of the flash.

Non-firing foot: The weak-side foot. For the left-handed shooter, it is the right foot and opposite for the right-handed shooter.

Pie off: Movement technique to look around visual barriers incrementally; also called the seven-meter side step.

Pistol: An autoloading firearm that has a short barrel and can be held, aimed and fired with one hand. A revolver uses a rotating cylinder, typically with six chambers. A pistol is magazine-fed.

Position Four: The fourth step in the presentation of the pistol. Refer to Chapter Six - Shooting Positions.

Position One: The first step in the presentation of the pistol. Refer to Chapter Six - Shooting Positions.

Position Three: The third step in the presentation of the pistol. Refer to Chapter Six - Shooting Positions.

Position Two: The second step in the presentation of the pistol. Refer to Chapter Six - Shooting Positions.

Presentation: The movement from position three to position four. This motion is straight toward the target, like on a rail system, so engagements may be conducted if needed before you are at full presentation.

Principle: A fundamental law, doctrine or assumption; also known as specific and/or broad doctrinal rules that always apply and do not change with the situation. These principles can be accomplished with various tactics given different factors (METT-C for you military types). Examples are 360-degree security and over-watch.

Press check: The act of insuring that your chamber is loaded after you load your pistol. With your finger off the trigger, pull the slide slightly to the rear and see the brass of the casing being pulled from the chamber. At night you will have to feel for the casing to ensure it is there.

Prone position: The position taken when lying on the ground. Refer to Chapter Six - Shooting Positions.

Ready position: The tactical resting position that is identical to position three of the presentation. Key points to this position are that the pistol is ready for use under the dominant eye and the front sight is visible with the peripheral vision.

Recoil spring: The spring in the pistol that returns the slide forward after the pistol has fired.

Rhythm drill: This drill is used to develop a smooth rhythm, speed, accuracy and the proper follow-through and recovery.

Round: Another word for cartridge.

Safety catch: Also called the safety. The mechanical device designed to reduce the chance of accidental discharges. Most disengage or block the firing pin when engaged.

Semi-automatic: A pistol which fires a single round each time the trigger is pulled, extracts and ejects the empty case, and inserts a new round into the chamber.

Shooting while wounded: The act of shooting while only using one arm because the other is injured. Refer to Chapter Ten - Shooting While Wounded.

Sights: Mechanical, optical or electronic devices used to aim firearms.

Simunitions FX: Brand of training ammunition that uses a non-lethal pellet filled with colored soap for marking of shots.

Single-action: A pistol action type that only releases the hammer when the trigger is pulled.

Slide: The moving part of the pistol on top of the action that removes a round from the magazine and inserts it into the chamber. The extractor on the slide pulls the round from the chamber, and it is then ejected from the pistol as the slide is forced to the rear.

Slide lock: When your pistol is shot until it is empty and the empty magazine locks the slide to the rear.

Slide release: Mechanical part of your pistol that is used to lock your slide to the rear when the magazine is empty. Release the slide from slide lock by pushing straight down on the slide release.

Slingshot: A slang term for a technique of closing a locked-to-the-rear slide. The slide is gripped at the rear serrations with your non-firing thumb and index finger and pulled to the rear; then this grip is released to allow it to return forward by its own spring tension. If you use the "slingshot" technique, pivot the pistol on the bore (right-handed shooters pivot the slide to the left) to have the slide meet your non-firing hand. Grasp the rear serrations of the slide, pull the slide slightly rearward and release. Regrip into your two-handed grip as you roll your sights back up and present back to the threat.

Slow-aimed fire: Deliberate slow fire using sights when great accuracy is needed and time is available.

Speed reload: The speed reload is used when you have shot all the rounds in your pistol and your slide is locked to the rear. Refer to Chapter Seven - Reloading Techniques.

Squib: A round which develops less than normal pressure or velocity after ignition and sometimes does not leave the barrel after a soft "pop."

Standing position: This position is the most common shooting platform and is detailed in Chapter Six - Shooting Positions.

Stovepipe malfunction: See failure-to-eject malfunction.

Strong-hand shooting: This position is used to fire your pistol with only the strong shooting hand. It may be used when you are shooting while wounded or while holding something that is obviously more important than your steady two-hand shooting grip. Refer to Chapter Six - Shooting Positions.

Supported position: The use of an object to steady your shooting position. Refer to Chapter Six - Shooting Positions.

Tactical reload: The tactical reload is used to reload your pistol with a fully loaded or almost fully loaded magazine before you move or anticipate a renewed assault on your position. It is controlled so you will maintain control of the magazines, the one being replaced and the one replacing it. Refer to Chapter Seven - Reloading Techniques.

Target fixation: Watching a target for a reaction when you should be analyzing or scanning to see if other threats are present.

Target indexing: The moving of your pistol from target to target. Multiple targets require some thought as how to engage in a prioritized order. Avoid target fixation or watching a target for a reaction when you should be engaging another target.

Tactic: An approach to a complex problem using the implementation of a specific set of techniques, allowing an individual or group to remain within the principles of an established doctrine.

Technique: A method of accomplishing a simple or basic task; it is developed independently, on a micro level, as the most efficient or effective method given a specific set of circumstances.

Trigger guard: Located on the underside of the frame, protecting the trigger from accidental discharges.

Trigger: The trigger is located on the lower part of the frame. When the trigger is pulled, it activates the hammer or the internal firing mechanism which, when released, causes the firing pin to strike and fire the round.

Weak-hand shooting: This position is used to fire your pistol with only the weak non-shooting hand. It may be used when you are shooting while wounded or practicing the same. Refer to Chapter Ten - Shooting While Wounded.

Weapon retention position: This position is used when you encounter an immediate threat within three feet and the threat is offensive. Refer to Chapter Nine - Combat Marksmanship.

SINGLE-ACTION PISTOL NOMENCLATURE

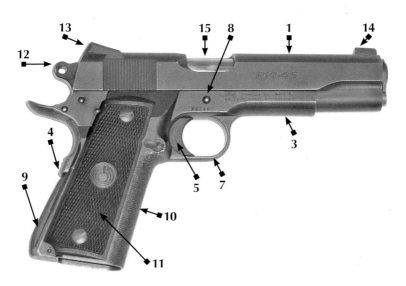

1. Slide
2. Slide release
3. Frame
4. Grip safety
5. Trigger
6. Safety
7. Trigger guard

8. Takedown pin
9. Backstrap
10. Front strap
11. Grip panel
12. Hammer
13. Rear sight
14. Front sight

15. Ejection port
16. Magazine release button
17. Magaine well
18. Muzzle

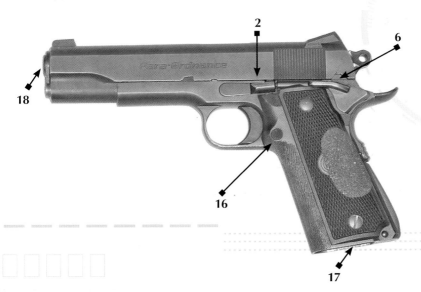

DOUBLE-ACTION/SINGLE-ACTION PISTOL NOMENCLATURE

1. Slide
2. Slide release
3. Frame
4. Decocker lever
5. Trigger
6. Takedown lever
7. Trigger guard
8. Backstrap
9. Front strap
10. Grip panel
11. Hammer
12. Rear sight
13. Front sight
14. Ejection port
15. Magazine release button
16. Magaine well
17. Muzzle

GLOCK SAFE-ACTION PISTOL NOMENCLATURE

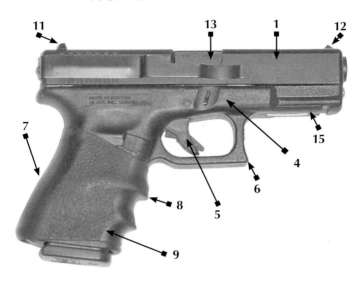

1. Slide
2. Slide stop
3. Trigger safety
4. Frame
5. Trigger
6. Trigger guard
7. Backstrap
8. Front strap
9. Grip panel
10. Takedown lever
11. Rear sight
12. Front sight
13. Ejection port
14. Magazine release button
15. Accessory rail
16. Magazine
17. Muzzle

CHAPTER THREE

SAFETY CONCERNS

When dealing with weapons, safety can never be forgotten. The more professionally an individual deals with his weapon and applies constant safety considerations, the more he shows his competence to others. Reckless handling of your weapon and lack of regard for what weapons are capable of doing quickly show when you are being observed on the range. This observation is another one you must make when you are maintaining your situational awareness. If you cannot safely handle your weapons, chances are you are just as inept at firing them. You must also take the responsibility for proper storage of weapons and their ammunition. Gun vaults, cable locks and trigger locks should be used when the situation dictates. Read and understand your manufacturer's operation and safety manual that came with your weapon.

Safety with handguns is one of the most critical aspects of handgun training. Because of the size and portability of handguns, they are prone to being pointed inadvertently in directions that the possessor does not intentionally desire. Often when an individual is addressed while holding a handgun, he or she will turn to face the person speaking and thereby accidentally point the pistol at that individual or some other unsuspecting person on the range. For that reason, shooters must be aware of the muzzle orientation of their pistol at all times, keep their finger off the trigger unless firing the weapon, and if at all possible, safe the pistol and return it to the holster or render it safe and point it in a safe direction when interacting with others that are not hostile.

"Range-ism"

There is often confusion between what I will refer to as "administrative protocol" and "weapons safety." Administrative protocol, or a "range-ism," consists of what each range institution has decided it will or will not allow and generally consists of guidelines on how it wants training conducted. Some of these are safety oriented, but more often than not, they are designed to limit the range of actions that can be taken by a shooter and thereby not give that shooter the opportunity to make a mistake.

The practical downside to most of these restrictions is that they do not coincide with combat-oriented training and shooters learn to act only if directed to do so and begin to stop thinking independently for fear of being reprimanded. They will wait to be directed and conduct actions that often defy common sense without a second thought, and that action creates a substantial safety risk. Having witnessed several accidental discharges and shooting incidents, I have heard the three statements you will hear before anything else: "I didn't think…, I didn't know…, I didn't see…." The one that covers it all is "I didn't think." When you direct someone not to think on his own, often he stops thinking altogether and just follows commands robotically. That is where the safety hazard is hidden.

A perfect example of a "range-ism" is the clearing procedure on most ranges. Often you will see shooters told to drop the magazine from the weapon onto the ground instead of dropping it into their hand and transferring it into a pouch or pocket. This is done for one of two erroneous reasons:

1. The institution does not trust the shooter to control a magazine in one hand and a pistol in the other; to that I respond, if one can't safely do that, one shouldn't have a pistol in the first place.

2. "If they drop the magazine in their hand, then they'll do it in a gunfight."

This is based on the Newhall incident in 1970, where four California Highway Patrol officers were killed by two heavily armed criminals. There have been contradictory stories as to whether or not the officers had been found with empty brass in their pockets. If so, this is very likely attributable to putting the expended cases in the shooter's pocket to avoid range cleanup, a range habit that in years gone by was all too common when shooting revolvers. The point is good training does not mean doing all things only one way; it means doing all things the logical way. There is no reason, at the close of a shooting evolution when the line has been administratively directed to go cold, that a shooter must drop a magazine to the ground. There are verbal and physical cues that reinforce the administrative clearing action, and that is distinctly different from an actual tactically oriented shooting drill. Remember, when you go "admin" (administrative), that means there is no constraint of time or tactical necessity; i.e., you're not on the clock and nobody is shooting at you. As long as there are distinct cues in your training that are reinforcing situation-appropriate actions, there is no need for protocol-driven range practices that are of no benefit.

The primary safety on any weapon is not the mechanical one; it is your brain attached to your shooting index finger, which will be resting along the pistol's frame until it is placed on the trigger when you decide to shoot. The finger is placed on the frame so there is less of a chance of an accidental discharge of the weapon. An accidental discharge may be caused by a reactive clinching of the muscles when you are surprised. This can happen if your finger is on the trigger or trigger guard. It can't if your finger is on the frame.

The following safety considerations are suggestions. You should use some or all of them when the situation dictates. Always use common sense when handling firearms and do not sacrifice quality training because it is too dangerous in the eyes of the untrained.

Weapon Safety

A. Treat all weapons as though they are loaded, regard-less of their condition.

B. Never point a weapon at anything you are not willing to kill or damage.

C. Keep your weapon on safe and finger off the trigger until your sights are aligned and you make the conscious decision to fire.

D. Know your target, foreground, background, left and right. Be aware of the ballistic capability of your weapon and the backstop.

"Down Range"

Down range is an administratively designated area where projectiles are intended to impact. Conditions and range status will identify it is a direction where a weapon may or may not be safely pointed and discharged.

"Safe Direction"

A safe direction by definition is a direction in which a weapon is pointed where a negligent or accidental discharge cannot harm personnel or equipment.

Down range is not always a safe direction!

NOTE: When using the double-action pistols, I teach students to decock them and leave their safety in the fire position because they are using the trigger finger as the primary safety, allowing them to smooth out their draw. It is a safe method when practiced and rule "C" listed above is not violated. For single-action weapons, the safety is on until they are oriented towards the threat in their shooting sequence. After engagements, the trigger finger comes off the trigger, the double-action is decocked and the decocker is returned to the fire position. The single-action is put back on safe. It is essential to practice each time in order for it to become a reflex.

Firing Line (Flat Range)

- Keep the pistol holstered, except when on the firing line or told to do otherwise by the instructors.
- Stay in line with other shooters.
- Never turn around with a pistol in your hand. Holster it first and then turn.
- Never dangle a pistol in one hand.
- Always use eye and ear protection.
- Take your finger off the trigger and out of the trigger guard when moving off target.
- Never shoot a target up range (opposite the direction of fire) or outside of designated range boundaries.
- Use the designated weapon-repair area to correct weapon deficiencies.
- Do not load until told to do so.

Range Procedures

- Always have some form of medical bag and know its location while you are at the range.

- Know the location of a cellular phone with the emergency numbers preprogrammed and a fill-in-the-blank form to include the who, what, when and where information the EMS operator will require when assisting you.

- The primary instructor clears weapons when leaving the range for the day.

- Pay attention to other shooters and use common sense with range etiquette.

- Never move down range without clearance from other shooters.

- Do not shoot objects not designated as targets.

- Shooters will clear malfunctions if possible. If not, call for the primary instructor.

- Keep your finger off the trigger while conducting reloads and malfunction correction drills.

- Anyone can call a cease fire if he or she sees an unsafe act.

Range Commands

"Load and make ready"

- Lock the slide to the rear.
- Place the magazine in the weapon.
- Chamber a round.
- Press check and decock or engage the safety.

Figure 3-1

Step One: *Lock the slide to the rear by pulling the slide to the rear and pressing up on the slide release/slide lock. Once it is engaged, release the slide tension.*

Step Two: *With the pistol pointed in a safe direction, insert the loaded magazine into the magazine well. Refer to Figure 3-2. Fully seat the magazine with the heel of the hand to ensure it is locked in by the magazine release. Refer to Figure 3-3. Your palm should be hard, as your fingers should be extended, not relaxed.*

Figure 3-2

NOTE: Note the shooter is keeping the pistol close to his body, which provides him much more dexterity than with his arms extended or at his waistline. Index your elbows on your ribcage to maintain consistency in your actions. Think "eye, muzzle, target" to keep the correct alignment to save time on the re-engagement. Think of where you thread a needle, and this is about where you

Figure 3-3

Figure 3-4

Figure 3-5

need to perform reloads and malfunction corrections.

Step Three: *With single-action pistols, you must pull the slide (by gripping the serrations on the rear of the slide, not over the ejection port) to the rear and release it to slam shut by its own spring tension. Refer to Figure 3-4. Return the pistol's safety catch to the safe position. An alternative method is to press down on the slide release and allow it to shut by its own spring tension. Refer to Figure 3-5. Return the pistol's safety catch to the safe position. Ensure the slide is in battery (fully forward).*

With double-action pistols, you can pull the slide to the rear while the pistol's safety is engaged and release it to slam shut by its own spring tension or press down on the slide release and allow it to shut by its own spring tension. Ensure the slide is in battery (fully forward).

Step Four: *Perform a press check to guarantee your chamber* is loaded. Figures 3-6, 3-7 and 3-8 are three techniques to perform a safe press check; ensure your finger is off the trigger. To perform a press check on a single-action pistol, you must disengage the safety catch, pull the slide back slightly so you may see the brass of the casing showing, release the slide and place the pistol back on safe. Do not pull the slide back too far because this action will make the pistol eject the loaded round. On the double-action pistol, you do not have to disengage the safety catch, so you just have to pull the slide slightly to the rear and see the brass casing. Refer to a Figure 3-8. Some of the newer pistols have a loaded chamber indicator; see your pistol manufacturer's instruction booklet. If there is a lot of tension on the slide, you may have to cock the hammer to press check and then decock if needed. At night you will have to feel the casing with a non-firing finger.

Figure 3-6

Figure 3-7

Figure 3-8

"Make Weapon Safe"

Decock, holster or engage the safety of the pistol and point it in a safe direction.

This could be a command to reholster also.

"Clear Your Weapon"

- Engage the safety. Utilize the particular safety your weapon has and remove the magazine while the muzzle is oriented in a safe direction.

- Pull the slide to the rear and lock it with the slide release. Allow the round to fly out – observe round being ejected; do not try to catch it. Pick it up once you have successfully cleared your weapon.

- Inspect the empty magazine well (see the ground through the magazine well).

- Inspect for an empty chamber—TWICE!

- Release slide without allowing it to slam shut by its own spring tension.

- Safe, holster and/or case weapon.

Step One: *Remove the magazine; put the pistol on safe. Refer to Figure 3-9.*

Step Two: *Pull the slide to the rear and lock it with the slide release. Refer to Figure 3-10. Allow the round to fly out–observe round being ejected; do not try to catch it. Pick it up once you have successfully cleared your weapon.*

Figure 3-9

Figure 3-10

Figure 3-11

Step Three: *Inspect the empty magazine well (see the ground through the magazine well). Refer to Figure 3-11.*

Step Four: *Inspect the chamber–TWICE! In low-light situations, you may physically have to feel into the chamber with your pinkie finger. Refer to Figure 3-12.*

Step Five: *Release slide without allowing it to slam shut by its own spring tension.*

Step Six: *Place the pistol on safe and then holster and/or case weapon.*

Figure 3-12

CHAPTER FOUR

BODY MECHANICS & PISTOL SHOOTING

Kinesiology is the study of the principles of mechanics and anatomy in relation to human movement. This chapter will discuss and clarify basic body mechanics as it relates to an effective shooting style. Before we continue, there are a few definitions that should be addressed.

Instinct: Instinct is the inherent disposition of a living organism toward a particular behavior. Instincts are unlearned, inherited fixed-action patterns of responses or reactions to certain kinds of stimuli.

Learned patterns of response: A learned pattern of response is an action that has been learned, and over time has become so rehearsed that it appears to be automatic or "instinctive" (automated neural control). Startled response or flinch response is a good example of a learned pattern. Humans learn when startled to protect their face with their hands, and although that appears to be an instinct, it is actually a learned behavior. When humans are startled and have made that decision to face what they perceive as a threat, they square their body to the threat in somewhat of a crouch. This position allows them to bring to bear the entirety of their vision, along with their arms, legs and teeth if the need arises to fight.

Economy of motion: This principle is physical efficiency creating maximum work. Often used as an analogy is the geometry definition, "The shortest distance between two points is a straight line." In layman's terms, it is the most amount of work with the least amount of effort. Because of the need to maximize scarce resources like money or food, humans learn as they progress to maturity to create the most amount of benefit with the least amount of effort, satisfying the desire to avoid wasted energy. For this reason, we are predisposed to efficiency in most every facet of life: We plan vacations, shopping trips, weekend chores, etc. Economy of motion is the hallmark of efficient weapons handling. Because it is a learned pattern, economy of motion can and should be continually refined in every training session.

Critical Patterns of Response

Several learned patterns of response are important to an effective shooting style.

Maintaining Balance

One of the first skills a child must learn is the ability to balance, and with that comes the ability to walk. This is a learned skill, but over time becomes so rehearsed that it appears to become "instinctive."

Body Positions For Strength, Dexterity And Visual Acuity

Because our safety often revolves around the ability to control our body movements, we learn through experience to adopt postures that give us stability, mobility and strength relative to the perceived situational needs. What is most efficient for humans in their day-to-day activities is to function at the intersection of strength and dexterity and also the intersection of manual dexterity and visual acuity. In simple terms, this state is your most effective range of motion and focal length for the task at hand.

For this reason, we believe the modified isosceles stance is the most stable and natural technique for a combat pistol shooter. It allows the shooter to take up generally the same type of stance a boxer or football player would use.

Both of those sports put a premium on stability and mobility in all directions, as should a combat pistol shooter. It also allows the shooter to face square to his target as he would do naturally, giving the added benefit (if wearing body armor) of having his armor cover the maximum amount of critical surface area, while not exposing a far more lethal oblique shot. The Weaver stance, aside from violating the learned response of facing a threat and mitigating some of the benefits of body armor, creates muscular tension that pulls a shooter out of his natural range of motion and thereby violates the concept of stability, mobility and strength.

Co-opting Body Motions

Since we adopt postures that give us stability, mobility and strength, we will often enhance our efficiency by co-opting existing body motions that have proven successful. The benefits of co-opting existing body motions are threefold:

- They are easier to learn because you aren't really "learning" them, only adapting them to a different task.
- They are easier to master rapidly and consistently.
- They are easier to execute on demand under stress.

These are critical but rarely acknowledged concepts and are a great way to explain to shooters of all levels why certain techniques work best.

COMMON QUESTIONS

Here are a couple of common questions shooters will ask and their explanations based on body mechanics.

"How far out should I extend my arms when I shoot?"

That distance is simple to explain. Extend your arm as though you were going to shake hands. Now look at the slight bend in your elbow. Do the same when reaching to grab an item, for instance a pen, from someone handing it to you, and then reach to pick up a bottle of water off a table. You will notice that the bend in your elbow is almost identical. Because you are not only judging distance, but also desiring to maintain strength and control, you have the intersection of visual acuity, manual dexterity and strength. That slight bend in your elbow is the bend that should be present when you extend your pistol out to full presentation.

COMMON QUESTIONS

"How far back do I bring my pistol on a reload?"

There are many different opinions based on…many different opinions. Quantifying it is difficult--until now. All one needs to do is rotate the pistol back to where he can read the writing on the slide. That will be the point where visual acuity and manual dexterity intersect.

NOTE: *If you have a visual disability, the default position would be where you read with prescription reading glasses. Oddly enough, that is the exact same motion as taking a can of soup off a shelf and reading the contents. This motion is conducted countless times at countless angles when we pick up an item to examine it. Now we have co-opted a motion that operates at the intersection of manual dexterity and visual acuity.*

When teaching the reload itself, one need only tell the student to pull an object from his pocket and examine it, or take a cell phone from a belt carrier. That motion is nearly identical to a reload: The hand goes into the pocket or to the carrier and retrieves the item. As the hand clears the pocket or pouch, the elbow drops and rotates the hand to the default focal length (the point at which the relaxed eye focuses--imagine reading a book) in the center of the body.

Physical Factors

Five individual physical factors affect a shooting platform or style.

Size

The size of the shooter will determine grip and stance. A smaller shooter with smaller hands will hold a pistol differently and may need to have a more aggressive stance then a larger one. Though that is not a hard-and-fast rule, it is often the case.

Strength

The physical strength of the shooter will also affect the construction of a shooting platform. An example is that female shooters often do not extend their arms as much when they are at full presentation. This is more often than not due to actual arm strength, and is easily overcome by more experienced female shooters.

Ability/Disability

If a shooter has a particular disability, i.e., shoulder or back injury, he may not be able to assume a textbook stance, but gets as close as possible.

Visual Acuity

The ability to see one's sights and target will also affect a shooter with non-20/20, uncorrected vision. It may require the pistol to be held further or closer to the eye to acquire the necessary focus.

Comfort

Although this seems ancillary, comfort is important to consistency. If a position is uncomfortable, the shooter will continually be trying to find a comfortable position, and thereby compromise the consistency of his platform. This approach is usually caused by violation of one or more of the above four factors and is also seen when a new shooter buys a pistol that does not fit his hand. As he gets more experienced, he will begin to "fidget" with the gun from shot to shot in order to find a grip that feels good. That fidgeting creates tremendous inconsistency in the shooting platform and degrades accuracy.

Moving and shooting

Oftentimes, moving and shooting is taught as though it is an advanced skill, when in reality it is a basic skill that requires more practice. What do you really need to be taught about moving and shooting?

Pelvis Direction

The pelvis faces in the direction of travel and the body goes naturally/comfortably where the pelvis faces. If a shooter is twisting or turning his body, he is walking in an awkward manner and that will have a negative effect on stability and accuracy.

Knee Bend

Slightly exaggerated bend of the knees. Most who have been through a military or law enforcement shooting course have heard the term "Groucho walk." This is a reference to the comic Grouch Marx and his signature exaggerated walk. The goal of that image is to get shooters to exaggerate their steps in order to enhance their ability to manipulate their weight and control their center of gravity.

There is a better way to explain the technique, but we must first establish the pertinent components of walking. These components are posture, pace, gait and balance.

- Posture is the position or bearing of the body, whether characteristic or assumed, for a special purpose.
- Pace is the rate at which one takes steps.
- Gait is the length of the individual steps.
- Balance is stability produced by even distribution of weight on each side of a vertical axis.

When learning to shoot while on the move, students must understand that there are only minor variations to their normal posture, pace and gait to enhance balance and thereby exert better control.

From the modified isosceles shooting posture, as he steps off, the shooter need only *slightly exaggerate* the bend in the knees, lowering the shooter's center of gravity straight down. From the waist up, the stance remains unchanged from his static shooting position. This position will lower the center of gravity, allowing the legs to act as shock absorbers and facilitate more control of his body weight and avoid jerky movement or tripping over objects. That bend in the knees will also force him to walk heel-toe and exaggerate his steps as he walks so his feet will clear the ground.

In the end, the only change in posture that is really necessary is a slightly exaggerated bend in the knees. Next will possibly be a change in pace. For more difficult shots or less-experienced shooters, it may be necessary to take slower steps in order to maintain an acceptable level of accuracy. The final component is gait, and that will vary from shooter to shooter based on the five individual physical factors (size, strength, ability/disability, comfort and equipment). Understand you will never be able to hold the weapon perfectly still and centered. Accept the bounce, but use your posture, pace and gait to keep your shot group stringing vertically, not horizontally, in the critical areas for incapacitation. Horizontal stringing is a sign that the shooter's pelvis is not facing in the direction of travel and is forcing him to "waddle" as opposed to walking naturally.

Condensed, that concept comes out as the following description: **When moving and shooting, take up a good shooting stance and then, as you step off, create a slightly exaggerated bend in the knees and walk heel to toe as though you were sneaking up on someone. Adjust your pace and gate appropriate to your ability and the acceptable level of accuracy required.**

Anywhere from the neck to the pelvis, from the center of the spine and 1.5 inches to the right and left (a 3-inch band with the spine in the center) is called the "spine box." Shots within that space it have a very good chance of disrupting spinal function and rapidly incapacitating a human.

Some women may find shooting on the move a little more difficult based on their skeletal differences, i.e., the difference in their hip and pelvis format, but it is usually minor if any.

The idea of timing your shots to your steps is both unrealistic and awkward. Shooters must find their own "groove" and shoot when the sights are on target, not try to force the break of the shots to fit their pace.

NOTE: You will never be able to keep the pistol perfectly aligned on the center of the target, but most important is that most of the movement is up and down, not side-to-side. Unless there is an obvious disability present, side to side movement and the subsequent stringing of shots left and right are symptomatic of an improper or awkward walking sequence by the shooter. Just walk normally with a slightly exaggerated bend in the knees, and accurate shooting on the move becomes quite attainable.

CHAPTER FIVE

SHOOTING FUNDAMENTALS

Before we start learning the basic shooting fundamentals, we must determine the shooter's dominant eye.

Dominant Eye

The definition of the dominant eye is the eye that you use primarily to see details, with the assistance of the less-dominant eye. The shooter should always aim with his dominant eye yet keep his non-dominant eye open also. In normal binocular vision there is an effect of parallax, and therefore the dominant eye is the one that is primarily relied on for precise positional information. Only using one eye will also affect your 3-D depth perception and greatly reduce your peripheral vision. If the shooter is right-handed and cross-eye dominant, the shooter just orients the pistol under the left (dominant) eye at position three to four during presentation.

Figure 5-1A

Figure 5-1B

Figure 5-1C

To find out which eye is dominant, take this simple foolproof test.

- Extend both arms in front of your body. Refer to Figure 5-1A.

- Place the hands together, forming a small opening between them. Refer to Figure 5-1B.

- With both eyes open, look at a distant object through the opening that was formed.

- Keeping focused on the distant object, bring your hands back to your face. Bring them back until they touch your face. Refer to Figure 5-1C.

- The eye that the opening is over is your dominant eye. If you have doubt, repeat the steps to be sure of your dominant eye.

Figure 5-2A

Stance

This fundamental of shooting is always important; it is the foundation for your shooting platform. For combat-type shooting, the stance should be solid, yet potently ready for movement. This stance looks like a fist-fighter's stance. This stance should be very similar to your shooting stance for tactical carbines and shotguns and with the empty-hand martial arts. The less you have to change for different weapon systems, the more natural it will be. Make this stance a habit.

Feet

The feet should be shoulder-width apart. The non-firing foot is slightly forward of the firing foot (usually three to six inches) and is pointed to the target to be engaged. Your firing foot should be firmly planted and at up to a 45-degree angle outboard to provide you with balance.

Figure 5-2B

Weight distribution between the non-firing foot and firing foot should be 60/40 and focused on your toes (essential in recoil management). Refer to Figure 5-2a through 5-2d. Your weight should be centered over the balls of your feet. This position also allows for quick lateral or forward movement.

Natural point of aim is very important for beginning shooters, as it is where the body naturally points and is a good starting place so you are not correcting for other mistakes. You can find your natural point of aim by acquiring your stance oriented at the desired target, closing your eyes, presenting your hands toward the target as if holding a pistol, and then opening your eyes. At what are you oriented? If it is not the center of the desired target, move your firing-side foot slightly forward or backward to bring your natural aim point to the desired area. Repeat until your hands are oriented to the center of the desired target.

Figure 5-2C

Figure 5-2D

Figure 5-3

Knees

Your knees should be slightly bent and your upper torso leaning forward. When you assume this position, you absorb the recoil through your body, which will allow you to speed up engagements.

Elbows

Your elbows should touch the side of your body. Stand with your head and shoulders square to the target and your head erect.

Your stance must be comfortable, so make sure you attain it every time you start your practice. Refer to Figure 5-3. It is quick to move from, you present the strongest part of your body armor, if used, and you are facing the known threat so you can analyze your courses of actions with the most amount of information available.

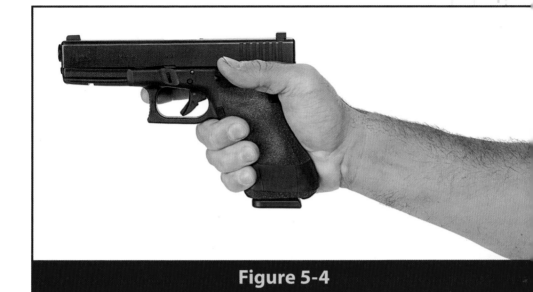

Figure 5-4

Grip

This section will teach a right-handed shooter who is right-eye dominant.

With your weapon pointed in a safe direction and the index finger off the trigger and outside the trigger guard, use the non-firing hand to place the pistol in the web of the shooting hand. Make a fist around the handle of the pistol. Your grip should allow you to place your trigger finger so that you have maximum control. Your trigger finger should be straight and lie along the side of the frame or the outside of the trigger guard. Refer to Figure 5-4.

Be sure to fit the "V" of your hand, formed by the thumb and the index finger of the shooting hand, as high as possible on the backstrap of the frame. This placement is to help manage recoil more efficiently. Your grip holding the pistol should align the backstrap of the pistol with the wrist and forearm.

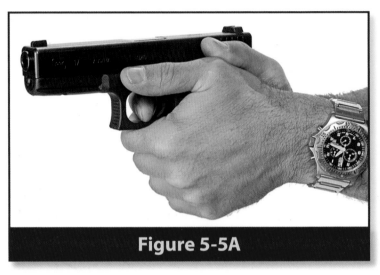

Figure 5-5A

Figure 5-5B

Your non-firing hand should now fill in the exposed grip panel from the back to the front to make a fist over your firing hand fingers. The thumb of your non-firing hand should be under the thumb of the firing hand, which is pushing down. The index finger of the non-firing hand should be indexed under the trigger guard, pushing up. Refer to Figure 5-5a and 5-5b..

Try to apply most of the tension to hold the pistol with your non-firing hand, which allows you to relax your firing hand and obtain greater control with your trigger finger. My rule is a 70/30 ratio of non-firing hand to firing hand tension. Others think that equal pressure (50/50) is more easily learned and works well for some.

Use 100 percent of the grip panels; you can use skateboard tape to maximize friction. Pinch the heels of your hands together to get a complete grip. If you have extremely white knuckles or start trembling immediately, you are gripping too hard. You must find your happy medium, for this balance allows for sustained shooting if the need arises. You will find the more you lock your wrists using the top tendon, the more control you have with recoil management.

The arms form two sides of a triangle, your back the third, with your arms taking equal pressure in your position. The elbows are just under a full lock (keep it comfortable) to assist in allowing the recoil to go through the arms into your chest to help manage recoil. You may have to modify this grip and your elbows slightly as everyone has different hands, physical dimensions, and different pistols have various grips. Your grip must be consistent and comfortable. This isosceles of the arms is more natural to maintain under extremes than some forms of the Weaver technique. Train to use your natural instincts, not to counter them.

NOTE: Your grip will change as you become more proficient, and you should always check your grip before drifting any sights. Pistols come from the factory bench sighted in, and you should make your hand fit your pistol, not your pistol fit your hand. If you do this step correctly, you will be able to shoot quite well with any factory, out-of-the-box pistol. Try different pistols to learn which one fits you the best; there are many different grip angles out there, so check them out first.

"Train to use your natural instincts, not to counter them."

Breath control

You must learn to hold your breath properly at any time during the breathing cycle if you wish to keep accuracy in stressful shooting situations. Remember that you must do this while aiming and squeezing the trigger. You must learn to inhale, then exhale normally, and then hold your breath at the

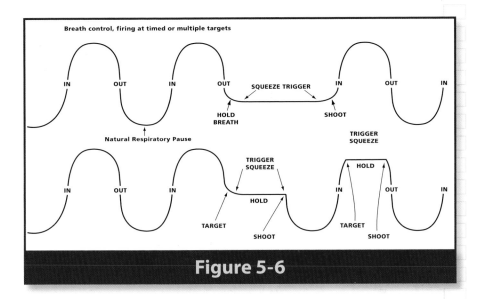

Breath control, firing at timed or multiple targets

Figure 5-6

moment of the natural respiratory pause. Refer to Figure 5-6. The top diagram is of a single shot and the bottom diagram is a series of shots.

This action allows you to steady your position with the front sight of the pistol at the precise aiming point while your breathing is paused. You must not hold your breath for more than five to seven seconds. The lack of fresh oxygen causes blurred vision and trembling muscles. Beginners will have to take a breath in between a multiple-shot drill, but with practice you will be able to shoot more with less breathing. Remember, this is one of the fundamentals, and once you start to shoot faster and under more stress you will have to manage your breathing and still get the job done.

Sight alignment and sight picture

I have combined these two considerations because they are very dependent on each other.

Sight Alignment

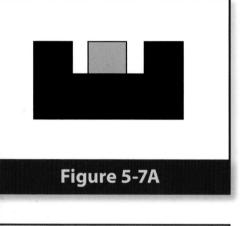

Figure 5-7A

Sight alignment is centering the front sight into the rear sight notch. The top of the front sight must be level with the top of the rear sight and in alignment with the eye. When you see this point, you will notice that on either side of the front sight is visible light. Your alignment must be such that the light on the left is equal to the light on the right. The eye will normally do this, but be aware of it when you start. Refer to Figure 5-7a.

Sight Picture

Figure 5-7B

Sight picture is taking this sight alignment and superimposing it onto your desired target. A correct sight picture is proper sight alignment with the front sight placed on the center of mass of the available target (your aiming point should be the size of the bullet you are firing). Remember that it is the center of mass of the available target, not a certain part of one's anatomy. If you see the whole person, it is his chest; if you see only his head, it is the center of that. Refer to Figure 5-7b. Since the eye can focus on only one object at different distances, you must focus on the front sight. Since the front sight is in clear focus (crystal clear with sharp edges and corners), your rear sight and target will be out of focus. Your front sight does not lie, so your bullet will go wherever your front sight was when you fired the shot. This point is handy in calling your shot, an educated guess as to where your bullet will go, since you saw the front sight lift off target when the pistol fired. You must keep both eyes open from the start of learning to shoot, thus allowing you to be more aware of your surroundings when you are aiming. You will need to begin using both eyes open because when you are stressed and in condition red, they will both be naturally open and not limiting your view. Train as you fight. Use your natural responses as you will have them with you.

Trigger control

Accurate shooting depends greatly on your control of the trigger. Trigger press and sight alignment must be done at the same time while maintaining the minimum arc of movement to attain accurate shooting. This fundamental is the most commonly violated, so take note and learn it correctly.

Single-action

First I will explain the single-action trigger control necessary to attain accuracy. The part of the index finger to be used is halfway from the tip to the first joint. This placement may change with time, as you will notice different bullet strikes when you place your finger differently on the trigger. Let's start with the beginner's trigger control. First you remove slack and apply initial pressure to the trigger once you are on your target. Settle into the aiming area and obtain the desired sight picture. Then begin applying a positive increase in pressure on the trigger, maintaining a smooth and even press to the rear without interruption. At first the shots should be a surprise to you. As you maintain your press to the rear, continue applying pressure on the trigger for a split second and release the trigger forward, only far enough to re-engage the sear, but do not allow your finger to lose contact with the trigger. Remove the slack and prepare for the next shot. It is paramount to concentrate on the front sight throughout the trigger press. Remember that where your front sight was when the shot was fired is exactly where your bullet will go. So it is good to focus on the front sight for accuracy and to know if you need to repeat the shot.

Double-action

Double-action is more difficult to learn initially, but it may become very effective if used with correct practice. The problem most people have when firing double-action is that they are fully extended towards the target when they begin to take the slack out and begin their press towards the rear with the trigger. This practice accounts for most shots being pulled to the right since the trigger pull of most double-action pistols is quite heavy.

To master fast and accurate double-action shooting, once you decide you are going to shoot you must begin to take out the slack (muzzle towards the target from position three) and begin the steady press to the rear as the pistol is brought from position three to position four, both hands on the pistol with it pointed towards the target. As you extend toward the target, you are removing the slack and applying increased pressure on the trigger to have the shot break as soon as fully presented. This action allows for very fast and accurate shots, since once the pistol is at full extension very little pressure is needed to make the pistol fire.

With practice this action will be as fast as a single-action. This technique also allows you to begin shooting once you are at position three and fire as you present the pistol to full extension. This technique is for advanced double-action shooting but is easily learned safely through proper dryfire. If in doubt, do not conduct double-action firing as described. Fully present to the target and have a smooth and steady press to the rear of the trigger as you attain a proper sight picture on the target.

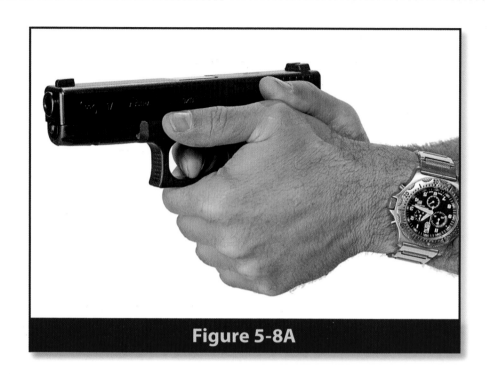

Figure 5-8A

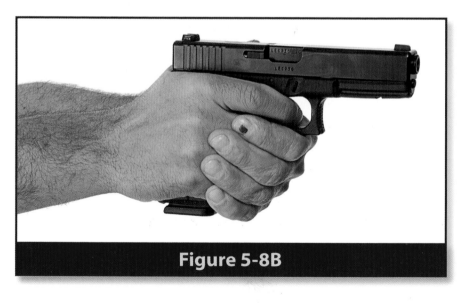

Figure 5-8B

Glock Safe-Action System

Think of this trigger action like a light double-action; learn how far you can press the trigger to the rear before it will fire. Practice the timing of the sights, extending your arms and the rearward trigger pressure. Notice the trigger finger does not touch the frame or trigger guard. Refer to Figures 5-8A and 5-8B.

NOTE: With either type of trigger, ensure that your trigger finger contacts the trigger only and not the frame, as it will move your bullet strike.

Follow-through

This step is the act of continuing to apply all the shooting fundamentals mentioned above throughout the break of the shot to prevent any unnecessary movement before the bullet leaves the barrel. The slightest movement will have a dramatic effect on your bullet strike. You should maintain concentration on sight alignment even after the shot has been fired. If you do this step correctly, you will achieve a surprise shot with no reflexes of anticipation to disturb your sight alignment. Within follow-through is the act of recovery, the act of returning the pistol to the original holding position in the aiming area. If you use the proper stance, grip and arm position, the recovery will be more natural and uniform.

Proper recovery must be accomplished as quickly as possible by taking the recoil straight back from the pistol to the shoulders. As soon as the shot breaks, you must immediately resume the sequence of applying the fundamentals for the next shot (manage recoil, reacquire another sight picture, reset the sear [letting the trigger out just far enough to reset the sear, which allows the pistol to be able to fire again], and prep the trigger [learn how far the trigger can be pressed to the rear before it will fire] for a follow-up shot if needed). Think of follow-through three ways: mentally (your thought process of what happened and what is happening), physically (discussed above as how to get the pistol back on target ready to re-engage), and tactically (what should I be doing to survive the engagement?).

Conclusion

These shooting fundamentals are just the basic instruction needed to continue with more advanced pistol learning. The coach-pupil method of teaching works well with these techniques if the teacher is knowledgeable in the application of the techniques. At this point, you may have to enlist an instructor because no book can see what you are doing incorrectly. Remember to dry fire five times for every one live fire practice; there is no need to waste your training resources on incorrect techniques. Ensure your pistol is clear before conducting dry-fire practice.

Follow through includes three aspects: mental, physical, and tactical.

CHAPTER SIX

SHOOTING POSITIONS

This chapter explains the proper draw from a holster, various shooting positions and their uses. It begins with the steps to the full presentation from the holster, otherwise known as the draw sequence. It is broken into four steps. Each step is important for its own reasons, so it is essential to practice them exactly so they become reflex. The draw is essential to all other practical combat shooting.

Figure 6-1A

Draw Sequence to Full Presentation

Position One

A threat is perceived and you decide you are going to draw and shoot, so you orient your stance towards the threat and begin your draw sequence. Quickly, your firing hand moves to form its grip on the pistol grip; this is the only chance to get a proper grip. Index with the web of the firing hand high on the backstrap (set your firing hand as high as you can on the backstrap), extend the trigger finger straight and then grip the pistol with the three lower fingers. Refer to Figures 6-1A and 6-1B.

The thumb disengages the thumb break on the holster and then finishes forming the grip as you begin to pull the pistol from the holster. The non-firing hand is drawn to the body's centerline and is open to receive the pistol with fingers extended and joined, oriented 45 degrees down.

Move only what you must to accomplish these steps of the draw. Econ-

Figure 6-1B

omy of effort and economy of motion allow you to do this quickly. Once you are comfortable with the correct step one, this step can be done as fast as possible as it is not a fine-motor function. This step is conducted at the fastest speed you can correctly do it.

Position Two

Your firing hand has its proper grip on the pistol and you draw the pistol from the holster. As soon as the pistol is clear from the holster, it is immediately pointed in the direction of the threat while moving to the centerline of the body to meet the non-firing hand. Refer to Figures 6-2.

The trigger finger can begin to take up slack in the trigger if you need to fire from the position of retention or an advancing threat at close ranges. As soon as you are pointing the muzzle at the threat, you can take the pistol off safe. As you move to position three you may orient the pistol under your dominant eye to assist in picking up the front sight faster. Refer to Figure 6-3A. The speed of this step is also as fast as possible once properly learned.

Figure 6-2

Figure 6-3

Position Three

Your non-firing hand begins to complete the two-handed grip and the muzzle is directed toward your threat. In this position, the finger is still off the trigger unless you intend to begin shooting. If the threat is closing or taking offensive actions and is within in your ability range, you may begin to engage from this position as you complete your presentation. This is the preferred ready position, with your finger off the trigger. The upper body must be semi-relaxed; watch tensing your trapezoids. Refer to Figure 6-3. Also, do not hunch your head forward; keep it naturally erect to a slight bit forward (keep it comfortable).

NOTE: From position three to four, the slack and tension are taken out of the double-action pistols. At full presentation is the point when the shot should break and fire to attain great accuracy and speed.

NOTE: The pressing of the hands and pistol forward from position three to position four is at a medium speed (allowing you time to press your trigger and acquire the sight picture desired). Smoothness must be emphasized to time the shot correctly at full extension—the trigger press, movement, sight alignment and sight picture all come together at full extension with a properly placed shot.

Position Four

This position is considered full presentation, and your most accurate shooting will be done from this position. Refer to Figures 6-4. If you have time, review your shooting fundamentals before the shot. Do not maintain this position for long unless the situation requires it. Optimum time is no more than six to eight seconds after your engagement.

Figure 6-4A

Figure 6-4B

"Actually see and analyze what is happening."

Once the engagement is complete, remove your finger from the trigger (only if the problem has been dealt with; remember to reset the trigger in your follow-through if the engagement is not complete) and take a breath in and exhale. Then scan and assess the situation; you should lower your muzzle one to two inches and look with three eyes (your two and your muzzle) by turning your head left and then right and then back to center. Actually see and analyze what is happening—you must turn your head (to the left, to the right, or wherever you need to look) as you look so you break the tunnel vision that is common in high-stress situations.

When you bring the weapon back to position three, check the condition of your weapon (ensure it is in battery), decock and/engage the safety on your pistol, and then look over your shoulders to check behind you; this puts you in a good position if you must turn and engage or fight. To rest, go to the low-ready position or back to position three of the draw.

Low-ready Position

This position is used to assess a situation after you have fully presented, deemed the situation is slowing, or need to rest and assess. Refer to Figure 6-5A and 6-5B. Many use this for range practice as a position for resting between drills; this should not be done as a standard operating procedure. Use position three of the draw sequence. Refer to Figures 6-3A and 6-3B. I advocate using position three of the draw for resting and waiting, as you are immediately ready to begin to fire if necessary. In a shooting situation, it is used to remain ready and allow you to see what is in front of you yet be ready to engage very quickly. MUZZLE TOWARD THREAT OR THREAT AREA!

Figure 6-5A

Figure 6-5B

Figure 6-6A

Figure 6-6B

Kneeling Position

This position is very tactically sound since it may be used to hide behind available cover and you can come out from the left, right or over to engage threats. The position shown in Figure 6-6A allows the shooter to stand back up and move if necessary. The position shown in Figure 6-6B is good for distant threats when you are behind good cover and you can go to the prone position easily. You can also go down on either knee and maintain 90-degree angles with your legs for stability as in Figure 6-6A. When you go to this position from the standing position, all you need to do is replace your firing side foot with your knee to go quickly and consistently to a kneeling position.

You may also take a kneeling position, depending on which side your spare magazines are stored on your kit for easy reach. For shooting around cover you put the knee down on the side you are shooting around (shooting around to the right you would put your right knee down, this limits your exposure).

Figure 6-7A

Your body type has a lot to do with how you take a kneeling position or whether you take a kneeling position at all. Refer to Figure 6-7A to see a two-knee-down variation. You may also practice with the use of your primary weapon (shotgun or rifle) and work out how you want to take a kneeling position to allow for you to get your pistol if a transition is needed.

The kneeling position may also be taken to shoot a high-angle shot in a close and crowded situation to clear your area behind the target and bullet path if it were to pass through. Refer to Figure 6-7B.

Prone Position

This position is a very steady, low-profile position from which to fire. The key is to practice this technique as detailed and not become lazy. The rollover prone position places the firing arm in line with the body to provide maximum recoil management and low profile. If you need some height to get the correct sight picture, you can use one of

Figure 6-7B

your knees to raise the weapon. If you do it the old cowboy way (as in Figure 6-8B) and rest on your elbows, you lose your recoil management advantages of the position in Figure 6-8A. To go into a prone position from the standing or kneeling positions, place your non-firing hand on the ground slightly ahead of where you want your torso to lay and manage your descent to the ground.

Remember to practice getting to your magazines and correcting malfunctions in the prone positions. Both positions are quite useful for different situations; practice them to find which one works for you.

Figure 6-8A

Figure 6-8B

Figure 6-9A

Figure 6-9B

Drawing from a Seated Position

The draw from a seated position is the same as if standing. Notice that the draw sequence is identical to the standing draw. Refer to Figures 6-9A through 6-9D. Consistency equals accuracy.

Sitting Position

The sitting position can be used when the situation allows. You are limited in your mobility, but with the appropriate cover, it is a very steady position. Notice in Figure 6-10 that the bones of the elbow are resting

Figure 6-9C

Figure 6-9D

against the inside of the knee joint, skeletal support as opposed to using your muscles to hold the position. Using skeletal support allows you to maintain this position longer without suffering muscular fatigue. Remember, shooting over cover is not always the best utilization of the cover, but the situation also dictates your choices.

Figure 6-10

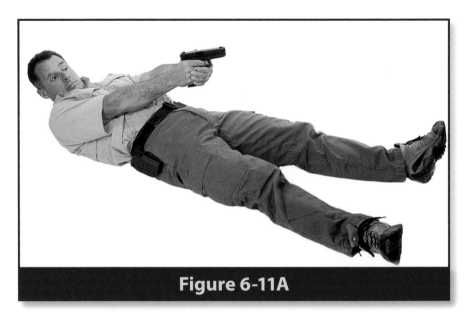

Figure 6-11A

Figure 6-11B

Supine Position

Supine shooting may be used when fighting from the ground, whether wounded or just off your base. Be careful to not shoot your own feet; lay them as flat to the ground as you can and be aware of their location if tracking a target. Refer to Figures 6-11A .

You may also use the bent-knee version of the supine position (Figure 6-11B); be aware of the location of your knees. Nothing hurts worse than a self-induced wound, mentally and physically. From this position, you can rotate on your back to re-orient to a new or moving threat as needed. It also allows your legs to assist in protecting your torso from direct impacts.

Figure 6-12A

Figure 6-12B

Strong-hand Shooting Position

This position is used to fire your pistol with only the strong shooting hand. It may be used when you are shooting while wounded or while holding something that is obviously more important than your steady two-hand shooting grip. With this position, you must turn your strong side toward the threat so that your arm is aligned with your chest. Notice the stance opens up with a slight step forward. Refer to Figures 6-12A and 6-12B. This stance puts the side of your chest behind your shooting arm. This position allows the recoil to be sent into your upper torso as you slightly bend towards your threat from the waist.

It is very important to tighten the wrist to unify your firing arm. Your pistol is slightly canted (45 degrees at most) to the left or as normally held—as straight up as normal. The 45-degree cant allows you to steady the pistol with the stronger muscles of your forearm and locks out your wrist to prevent it from bucking with recoil. You need to practice this position to determine your sight picture. Some may have to aim slightly low and to the right to hit their center of mass. While practicing or firing with a wounded non-firing arm, draw it up to your chest to steady your body's movement.

Weak-hand Shooting Position

This position is used to fire your pistol with only the weak, non-shooting hand. It may be used when you are shooting or practicing to shoot while wounded. With this position you must turn your non-firing side toward the threat so that your arm is aligned with your chest. Notice the stance opens up (refer to Figures 6-13A and 6-13B) toward the threat, which puts the side of your chest behind your shooting arm. This placement allows the recoil to be sent into your upper torso, which is slightly bent towards your threat.

Figure 6-13A

Figure 6-13B

Again, it is very important to tighten the wrist to unify your firing arm. Your pistol is slightly canted (45 degrees at most) to the right or as normally held—as straight up as normal. The 45-degree cant allows you to steady the pistol with the stronger muscles of your forearm and locks out your wrist to prevent it from bucking with recoil. You should practice this position to determine your sight picture. Some may have to aim slightly low and to the left to hit their center of mass. While practicing or firing with a wounded strong arm, draw it up to your chest to steady your body's movement.

NOTE: You will be moving in a modified position three, and when you need to shoot you will press to position four as if standing still. The exception to this is shooting at very close range using weapon-retention techniques. Trigger finger is off the trigger until you have intent to shoot.

Moving Forward

At times you should close in on a threat and not waste time stopping to take the shot. The key to moving and shooting is to move only as fast as you can effectively engage. This is explained as a "careful hurry."

When moving forward, use a heel plant and roll the foot to the toes and take the next step. Lower the body with some bend in the knees to act as shock absorbers. Refer to Figures 6-14A through 6-14C. You may also have to shorten your steps. You are trying to move from the waist down and not have your head bobbing as your weapon will also be bobbing.

This is a learned skill to build confidence to move quickly and still attain your desired accuracy. Continue to practice magazine changes

Figure 6-14A

Figure 6-14B

and malfunction drills while moving. Practicing when you actually break the shot (feet on ground or one in the air) must be decided upon by the shooter. You should not have to stop to fire effectively less than 25 meters on a full silhouette-sized target.

Figure 6-14C

Figure 6-15A

Figure 6-15B

Moving Backwards

No one likes to talk about moving backwards in a tactical situation, but sometimes it is necessary. We will not discuss why you are moving backwards, but the most sensible way to do so.

To maintain sight of an area or threat, you decide you do not want to lose security by turning and running. Identify where you are going and determine the best pace at which to get there. Study the ground for any obstacles and re-orient toward the threat area or threat and begin to move backwards by sliding your rearward foot along the ground, feeling for any obstacles that may cause you to trip and fall. Refer to

Figure 6-15C

Figure 6-15D

Figure 6-15A through 16-15D. Alternate feet until you get to where you want to go and continue with your plan; your forward foot should not slide past your planted foot.

Hazards of moving backwards are obvious and it should be conducted as safely as possible as the situation dictates.

Shooting Lateral To Movement

"You may decide you need to slow down at the break of the shot."

This can easily be done by just turning your upper body (your tank turret) toward the threat and engaging by rotating from the knees up. Refer to Figure 6-16a (strong side lean) and Figure 6-16b (weak side lean). You may decide you need to slow down at the break of the shot, but you should practice so you know how fast you may go to continue movement. If you begin to turn too much away from your direction of movement, you may have to turn toward the threat as the situation dictates. And depending on the situation, you may choose to shoot to the sides with a one-hand technique. The circumstances may require it. Survival modifies many learned skills.

Figure 6-16A

Figure 6-16B

Figure 6-17A   **Figure 6-17B**

Sidestepping

Sidestepping is used when you "pie off" (to look tactically around visual barriers incrementally, exposing minimal body parts) an area. Do not step across your feet as there is more of a chance of tripping over your own feet. Move the foot on the side you want to go in that direction and then bring your trailing foot over and continue. Refer to Figures

Figure 6-17C

Figure 6-17C

6-17A through 6-17D. This shooter is moving to his left. It is related to the slide and drag used to move to the rear. Do not lift your feet if you do not have to; slide them to avoid losing balance from contacting an obstacle.

Figure 6-18A

Muzzle Direction During Movements

If you are moving with your weapon in the low-ready or position three, you must be aware of where your muzzle is pointing. You can safely move this way *if* you pay attention to those around you who do not need a muzzle pointed at them. If a non-threatening individual is crossing your muzzle, bend your wrists down to orient the muzzle to the ground until he is out of the way and then bring the muzzle back up. Refer to Figure 6-18A and 6-18B.

Be very cognizant as to your muzzle direction. At no time should it be oriented at anything you are not willing to destroy. Practice this even with training weapons or dry rehearsals so it will be second nature. Those around you will appreciate it.

Turning 90 Degrees

You can turn 90 degrees while standing or moving in basically the same way. Pivot on the ball of the foot for the direction you want to turn and

Figure 6-18B

place the other foot in your normal stance once your turn is almost complete. Refer to Figures 6-19A through 6-19E. Why turn to begin with? You *perceive* a threat (so you turn your head to look), *recognize* it is a threat (begin your turn), and *acquire* the threat (with your sights) in preparation to shoot. This is a P.R.A. drill used to perceive, recognize and acquire a threat to one side or the other.

Figure 6-19A

Figure 6-19B

Figure 6-19C

Figure 6-19D

Turning 180 Degrees

Turning around 180 degrees is normally conducted from a static standing position and is similar to the 90-degree turn previously discussed. Refer to Figures 6-20A through 6-20D. This is a P.R.A. drill used to perceive, recognize and acquire a threat to the rear.

Remember, the direction you turn your head to look is the direction you will be turning your body. Refer to Figure 6-20A. And as with a 90-degree turn, you will pivot on the ball of the foot that you are turning (turning left - pivot on the ball of the left foot and vice versa for turning right). Refer to Figure 6-20B. Your outboard foot should come to a stop in the normal shooting stance so you are ready to engage as if you were already facing that direction. Refer to Figure 6-20C. If drawing during the turn, do not bring your muzzle horizontal to the ground until you are oriented toward the threat.

Figure 6-20A

Figure 6-20B

Figure 6-20C

Figure 6-20D

I also suggest using a Saf-T-Blok from Concept Development Corporation for use carrying the Glock pistol in this manner. The Saf-T-Blok reduces the possibility of accidental discharge when carrying unconventionally, like in a fanny pack, tucked in a belt or in your pocket. It snaps into place behind the trigger, providing a positive trigger block. And when the pistol is needed, it ejects instantly by pushing the Saf-T-Blok ejector with the index finger.

NOTE: This carry method has been employed as far back as the OSS and most recently by a Philippine terrorist group for assassination teams. This method has the individual carrying the pistol in front of his/her pants without a holster. The key point is to push up on the muzzle with the non-firing fingers to allow for acquiring a proper grip as you draw. Refer to Figure 6-26B. KEEP YOUR FINGER OFF THE TRIGGER UNTIL ON TARGET AND READY TO SHOOT.

Figure 6-26B

Concealed Draws

Figure 6-21A

Figure 6-21B

Figure 6-21C

Figure 6-21D

Figure 6-21E

Figure 6-21F

Drawing from a Cover Garment

When beginning to sweep the cover garment, it is better to start up high at the collar area and sweep in and down to avoid getting a handful of jacket instead of the grip refer to Figures 6-21A and 6-21B. Doing this also does not tip your hand if you are surprised and begin to draw and then decide not to. The only difference in drawing from concealment is getting to your pistol; other than that aspect, it is a normal four-step draw. Dry firing is the best way to practice a draw from concealment. You may have to try different carry methods, holsters, or pistols to find one with which you are comfortable and confident. Remember, you carry them more than you use them, so you must find a happy medium between comfort and practicality.

NOTE: To remained concealed, the holster and magazine pouches must remain behind your hip bone (kidney area carry) to prevent flashing your equipment during normal activities. Refer to Figures 6-22A and 6-22B. This also aids in immediate muzzle-to-target orientation as you are not twisting the sight up onto target.

Figure 6-22A

Figure 6-22B

Concealed Carries without Holsters

Figure 6-23A

Figure 6-23B

Figure 6-23C

Figure 6-23D

Figure 6-23E

Figure 6-23F

Untucked Shirt Draw

When the shirt is ripped up to allow the firing hand to get a grip, the non-firing hand is in the location needed to complete the two-handed grip at step three of a normal draw sequence. Ensure you slide your firing hand thumb well behind the pistol as you begin to form your grip, refer to Figure 6-23C. This is also a caution to watch suspects which take this posture and are preparing themselves the courage to draw, Figure 6-23B.

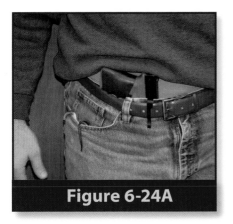

Figure 6-24A

Figure 6-24B

Obviously you do not want your trigger finger near the trigger as noted before or during the actual draw part of the presentation. This is a very good carry method for Glock with the Carry Clip from Skyline Toolworks with a Saf-T-Blok to immobilize the trigger during carry.

Figure 6-25A   **Figure 6-25B**

I also suggest using a Saf-T-Blok from Concept Development Corporation for use on carrying the Glock pistol in this manner. The Saf-T-Blok reduces the possibility of accidental discharges when carrying unconventionally, like in a fanny pack, tucked in a belt, or in your pocket. It snaps into place behind the trigger, providing a positive trigger block. And when the pistol is needed, it ejects instantly by pushing the Saf-T-Blok ejector with the index finger.

"Sparrow Team" Felony Carry

This carry method has been employed as far back as the OSS and most recently by a Philippine terrorist group for assassination teams. This method has the individual carrying the pistol in front of his/her pants without a holster.

Figure 6-26

Figure 6-26B

Figure 6-26C

Figure 6-26D

Figure 6-26E

Figure 6-26F

The key point is to push up on the muzzle with the non-firing fingers to allow for acquiring a proper grip as you draw. Refer to figure 6-26B. **KEEP YOUR FINGER OFF THE TRIGGER UNTIL ON TARGET AND READY TO SHOOT.**

CHAPTER SEVEN

RELOADING TECHNIQUES

The act of reloading is an over-looked issue in most training, but it is true that shooters are killed due to dropping magazines, shaking hands, placing the magazine in backwards and placing empty magazines back into the pistol. The stress induced by a life-threatening situation causes shooters to do things that they would not otherwise do. Consistent and repeated training—properly performed—is needed to avoid such mistakes.

- Develop a consistent method for carrying magazines in the ammunition pouches. All magazines should face down with the bullets facing forward and to the center of the body. Your pouches should properly secure your magazines during strenuous actions.

- Never practice an administrative reload. On the initial load, perform a speed reload. Be slow and technically correct to begin with and speed will come, but it is critical to practice with proper technique so as not to practice bad habits into routine.

- Know when to reload. When possible, perform the tactical reload; it is safer to reload with a round in the chamber to fire in an emergency. And you do not have to release the slide as when reloading from a slide lock. In a fight, reload when you can, not when you are forced to. Think tactically and ask yourself if you have the time and the opportunity to do it; if so, then perform a tactical reload.

- Obtain the proper grip on the magazine to be loaded. This grip precludes the magazine being dropped or difficulty in placing the magazine into the pistol. Use the index finger to guide the magazine into the pistol. You must force yourself to shift focus momentarily to ensure you put the magazine into the magazine well correctly every time.

Practice these techniques under some type of stress. It may be through competitions, noise, after physical exercises—whatever gets your heart to pound—and you will then have to learn to calm yourself.

Reloading the semi-automatic magazine-fed pistol is broken down into the tactical reload and the speed reload.

Tactical Reload

The tactical reload is used to reload your pistol—either with a fully loaded or almost fully loaded magazine—before you move or anticipate a renewed assault on your position. This movement is a controlled one, so you maintain control of both the magazine being replaced and the one replacing it. It should be performed from behind cover if tactically feasible and before you run out of ammo and experience a slide lock to the rear. Remember to think tactically and ask yourself if you have the time and the opportunity to do it; if so, then perform a tactical reload.

Step One: Once you have decided to perform a tactical reload, maintain security toward your threat area with the pistol and your eyes. Ensure your finger is off the trigger and, with your non-firing hand, properly draw a fresh magazine from your pouch. Refer to Figures 7-1A and 7-1B.

Figure 7-1A

Figure 7-1B

To draw a magazine properly, extend your index finger along the front (the side of the magazine that the bullets are pointing at) of the magazine. Once the magazine is out and on the way to the pistol reposition it so that the fresh magazine is between your index finger and the middle finger.

Step Two: While maintaining the proper grip on the fresh magazine, slightly rotate the pistol in your hand so you may push the magazine release to drop the used magazine. With your non-firing hand, pinch the used magazine with the index finger and thumb, and then withdraw the used magazine from the pistol. Refer to Figure 7-2A. You may have to shift your vision quickly to the pistol to ensure that the exchange is completed smoothly, but then you must reshift your attention back to the threat area.

While holding both magazines in the non-firing hand, insert the fresh magazine into the magazine well of the pistol. Maintain eye, muzzle and threat

Figure 7-2A

Figure 7-2B

alignment to speed and ease the re-engagement. Refer to Figure 7-2B. This action may not be comfortable for individuals with small hands and large-capacity magazines. Remember that under great stress this technique may be difficult to do, so you must practice until it is reflex-like.

Step Three: Once the magazine is halfway into the magazine well, firmly seat it with the palm of the non-firing hand. Notice where the pistol is in relation to your body; it maintains the eye, muzzle and target line to minimize movement and speed up your re-acquiring the sight onto target if needed. Refer to Figure 7-3A.

Once the pistol is loaded, stow the used magazine somewhere other than where you have the fully loaded ones—front pocket, back pocket, or a belt pouch—but do not keep it in your teeth or in your hand. Refer to Figure 7-3B.

Figure 7-3A

Figure 7-3B

Figure 7-4A

Figure 7-4B

Speed Reload

The speed reload is used when you have shot all the rounds in your pistol and your slide is locked to the rear. Unlike the tactical reload, which is moderately slow, the speed reload relies on speed to reload your pistol so you can continue the fight. Learning it will be done slowly so you perform the steps correctly; speed will come with practice. Keep a straight line with your eye, muzzle and target when you bring the pistol back toward your face so you can quickly and easily roll the pistol back onto target and pick up the front sight quickly.

Step One: When you realize that your slide is locked to the rear because it is empty, you must immediately shift the pistol in your strong hand so you may reach and activate the magazine release with your firing-hand thumb. At the same time, your non-firing hand will quickly go to the centerline of your body and move left along the belt to your magazine pouch. Refer to Figure 7-4B. With the non-firing hand index finger extended on the front of the magazine, pinch the first magazine you touch with your

Figure 7-5

thumb and middle fingers. Refer to Figure 7-5. This pinch allows you to control the removal of the magazine from the pouch and position it for insertion into the pistol.

Note: Your magazine pouch will determine how you execute this step. Refer to Figure 7-6A. If it is snapped or fastened with Velcro, incorporate this detail into the step to smooth out your magazine removal.

Note: If the magazine in the pistol does not drop, you will have to strip it from the magazine well. To do this step, you use the edge of the fresh magazine to put pressure on the baseplate of the stuck magazine. An alternative method is to pinch the stuck magazine with the pinkie and ring fingers, pull it out and drop it, and then continue to reload the pistol.

Step Two: Once the magazine has fallen from the pistol to the ground and the fresh magazine is on its way to the magazine well, with the magazine well rotated back toward your face, prepare to "thread the needle." Refer to Figure 7-6B. Ensure you can slightly see the open hole of the magazine well on your quick peek to ensure the magazine is going to hit the hole. Maintain your eye, muzzle and target alignment.

Figure 7-6A

Figure 7-6B

Figure 7-7A

Step Three: As you begin to insert the fresh magazine, glance at the magazine well to ensure the extended index finger guides the magazine into the well. Refer to Figure 7-7A. As soon as half of the magazine is in the magazine well, immediately refocus on the threat. Vigorously seat the magazine in the pistol with the heel of the non-firing hand, ensuring you have a hard palm with your fingers extended. Refer to Figure 7-7B. Disengage the slide release with your firing hand thumb and allow the slide to close by its own spring tension. Refer to Figure 7-7C.

Figure 7-7B

Figure 7-7C

Figure 7-8A

Figure 7-8B

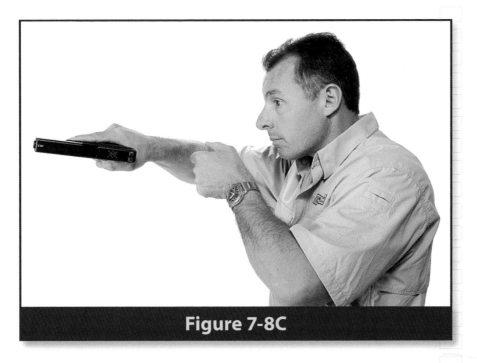

Figure 7-8C

An alternative may be for you to "slingshot" the slide by gripping the rear serrations of the slide with your non-firing hand's thumb and index finger and pulling the slide to the rear, then letting it return by its own spring tension. Refer to Figure 7-8-a through 7-8c. If you use the "slingshot" technique, pivot the pistol on the bore (right-handed shooters pivot the slide to the left) to have the slide meet your non-firing hand. Grasp the rear serrations of the slide, pull the slide slightly rear, and release. Regrip into your two-handed grip as you roll your sights back up and present back to the threat.

Figure 7-9

Step Four: Reform your grip and continue the engagement. Refer to Figures 7-9. If you keep your eye, muzzle and target alignment, it is simple to re-acquire your front sight quickly as you regrip. A good time for a speed reload (position three to four, one shot, reload and shoot) is 3 to 3.5 seconds on a full silhouette-sized target at seven meters, depending on the type of magazine pouch you are using.

Figure 7-10

Note: Refer to Chapter Six on the draw from concealment for sweeping motion to get back to your magazines every time so you can feed that hogleg. Figure 7-10 shows reloading from concealment.

CHAPTER EIGHT

MALFUNCTION DRILLS

Malfunctions are usually preventable through good practice, but they may still occur out of the blue from time to time. Of course, you hope it is on the practice range, but you should treat each one as if you are in a life-or-death situation. Practicing proper and effective corrective actions will allow you to be more confident in your pistol handling. If unprepared in stressful situations, you can become much more stressed due to an unforeseen malfunction that is easily remedied. I have observed many shooters that perceive themselves to be experienced, but when they encounter a stovepipe they nearly disassemble the pistol rather than sweep it out and continue.

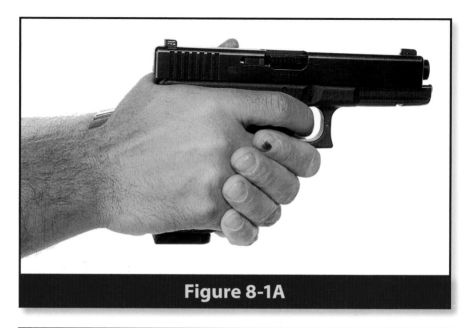

Figure 8-1A

Figure 8-1B

Proper training will do more to save your life than technology and the arms race to be bigger and better. Malfunction drills must fix the problem 100 percent of the time (excluding a weapon stoppage—broken weapon) the first time performed. You must look at the pistol and identify the problem. Obviously the pistol is not functioning as you need, so you must transition to another weapon or rectify the situation. It is a non-functioning weapon at this point—fix it.

Whether you take a kneeling position to correct malfunctions is up to you, depending on the situation or how you operate. If you do and others are around you with weapons, let them know you are going to stand back up by whatever means you have pre-arranged.

Note: The failure-to-go-into-battery malfunction, when your slide does not fully return forward when cycling a round, is always rectified in the same manner, no matter which hand is being used. This malfunction is usually induced when loading and not allowing the full recoil spring tension to shut the slide. Refer to Figure 8-1A.

To fix a failure-to-go-into-battery malfunction, ensure your finger is off the trigger and outside the trigger guard and then slap the back of the slide with the heel of the non-firing hand. Refer to Figure 8-1B. If you are shooting while wounded, then you will use your chest or equipment to force the slide forward into battery.

Figure 8-2

Failure To Fire

The failure-to-fire malfunction occurs when the operator has loaded a dud cartridge or failed to load the chamber. The universal fix all for this is the "Slap, Rack, Ready" technique.

Symptom

You perform a full presentation to shoot and hear and feel the hammer strike, but the weapon does not fire. Refer to Figure 8-2. Before performing this correction you must remove your trigger finger from the trigger.

Corrective Action: Slap, Rack, Ready

- SLAP the bottom of the magazine with a hard palm (fingers extended) to ensure it is fully seated and locked in. Refer to Figure 8-3A.

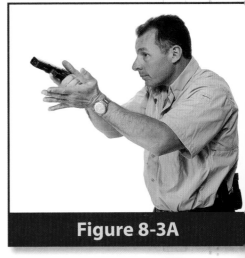

Figure 8-3A

- RACK the slide fully to the rear and release it to shut by its own recoil spring tension. You can pivot the slide toward your non-firing hand on the axis of the bore. This can speed up and assist in racking the slide to the rear. Maintain muzzle-to-threat orientation. Refer to Figure 8-3B.

Figure 8-3B

- READY or re-present and prepare to fire the shot as you intended before the malfunction if your situation dictates that action. Refer to Figure 8-3C.

Figure 8-3C

Tap-Rack-Roll (Which way and why?)

Many agencies and training venues have been teaching what is called tap-rack-roll, and if done in the manner I have described in the malfunctions chapter, it will accomplish the task of ensuring that a stoppage can drop free during immediate action on a Glock pistol.

First, I do not advocate rotating the hand around so that the thumb points back at the body unless it is being done in a confined space or there is a potential threat within arm's reach and retention is a serious concern. The reason I don't advocate that technique is that it is outside the normal range of motion; violates economy of motion; brings the gun much further off target; exposes the armpit, thereby compromising the armor protection (if being worn) or exposing the shooter to a more lethal oblique shot; and is slower. Another problem with the thumb pointing towards the body is that this grip obscures and possibly fouls the ejection port.

Rolling the pistol to the shooting side violates range of motion, economy of motion, and general common sense. I have heard some say it is a gross motor skill and the other way isn't––you are using the exact same hand format I advocate, but you are doing it outside of your natural range of motion while obscuring the ejection port and potentially compromising your armor. Another reason given for rolling the pistol to the shooting side is that the lower side of the port is facing the ground, and some say that position will more reliably allow a stoppage to fall free. Figure it out yourself: Lock the slide to the rear and see if an empty case or live round falls free if you turn the pistol slightly more than 90 degrees to the left. The three most common reasons to do tap-rack are failure to load a magazine into the pistol properly, inadvertent dislodging of a magazine, and/or a bad round. None of these is affected at all by rolling the pistol in any direction. The first two issues are that the pistol hasn't chambered a round, and in the last situation the chambered round is bad but the extractor has control of it.

The fastest way I have found, if a shooter is actively engaging and is not at arm's length or closer, is the method described in the malfunctions chapter. Rotating the pistol slightly more than 90 degrees towards the non-firing side will easily allow a stoppage to fall free, while going further than that only wastes time and takes you farther out of your natural range of motion.

Use the technique that best accomplishes the task. Know what you do and why you do it!

Think about every motion you practice and make sure you know why it is the best solution. In a close-range or contact-distance encounter, I would conduct tap-rack close to my body with my thumb pointed towards my chest. That is because once the pistol is brought in that close, it changes the body's functional range of motion and does not violate it; the other way is just too difficult because the hand working the slide has nowhere to go.

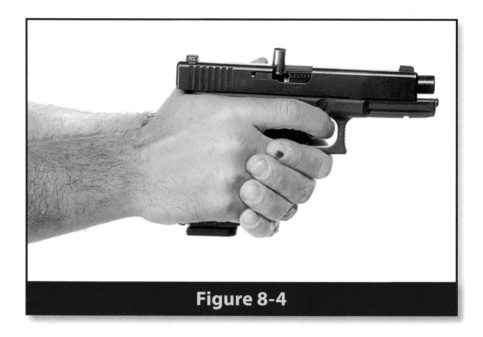

Figure 8-4

Failure To Eject

The failure-to-eject malfunction (commonly called a "stovepipe") is created usually by the slide being retarded by not setting one's wrists ("limp wristing") in its rearward movement to rechamber the next round or by a broken ejector. Refer to Figure 8-4. This malfunction is easily corrected by sweeping the expended case from the port. The corrective action is the same for vertical and horizontal stovepipes.

Symptom

You are in the act of shooting a multiple-round engagement and you notice you cannot see your front sight for a piece of brass in the way, know the slide did not fully close, and/or have a soft, mushy trigger. Refer to Figures 8-5A and 8-5B.

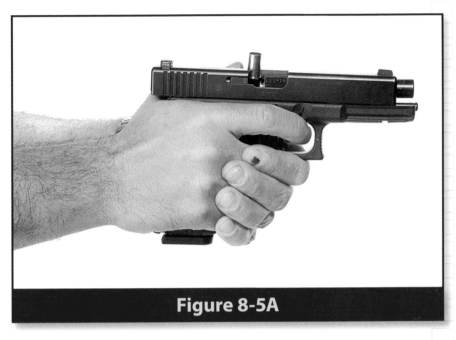

Figure 8-5A

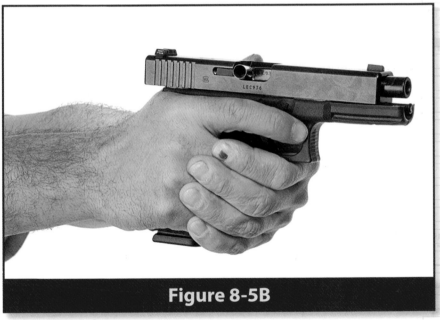

Figure 8-5B

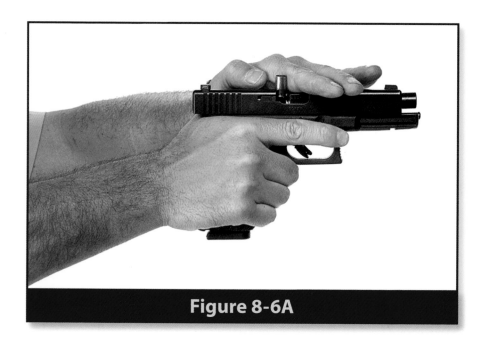

Figure 8-6A

Figure 8-6B

Corrective Action

With the non-firing hand, extend your fingers, and with fingers joined, reach over the slide. Refer to Figure 8-6A. DO NOT SWEEP YOUR HAND IN FRONT OF THE MUZZLE. Roll your fingers over the top of the slide, and with a firm, vigorous sweeping motion to the rear against the stuck casing, sweep it free. Refer to Figure 8-6B. Do not sweep this too far as you have to take more time to regrip and present.

Once the casing is no longer pinched by the slide, the slide will continue to seat the next round, and you are now ready to continue the engagement. Refer to Figure 8-6B. Many inexperienced shooters do too much to correct this simple malfunction. *Ensure you do not work the slide fully to the rear when sweeping the empty casing—this could induce a double feed as the chamber is already loaded.* Continue the engagement as your situation dictates.

Note: You must always roll your fingers across so that whichever malfunction you encounter, vertical or horizontal, you will clear it with one sweep.

Figure 8-7

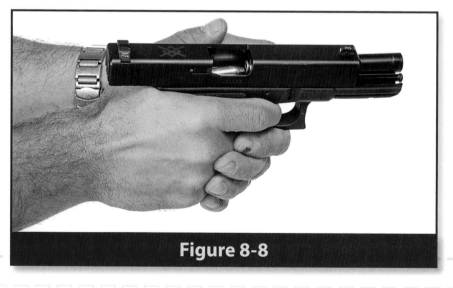

Figure 8-8

Failure To Extract

The failure-to-extract malfunction (commonly called a "double feed") is created when the spent casing is not extracted from the chamber, and the next round to be loaded is rammed from the magazine into the rear of the stuck casing. Refer to Figures 8-7 and 8-8. This malfunction is a serious one since dexterity and movement are needed to correct it and, of course, to do it quickly. Below is the breakdown of the corrective action to restore your pistol back to operation.

Symptom

You are shooting a multiple-shot engagement and notice your slide did not go forward; you have a soft, mushy trigger; and it will not fire.

Figure 8-9A

Figure 8-9B

Corrective Action

Step One: With your finger off the trigger, rotate the pistol in your firing hand so you may engage the slide release with your firing-hand thumb. With the non-firing hand, rack the slide to the rear and lock it with the slide release by pushing it up into the notch and let the recoil spring tension hold the slide release in the notch. Refer to FIGURE 8-9A. The slide is locked to the rear first so as to release the recoil spring's tension on the malfunction; this works every time to assist in correcting this malfunction.

Step Two: Remove the magazine from the pistol. Refer to Figure 8-9B.

Step Three: Rack the slide to the rear at least two times to ensure the casing is extracted and ejected from the pistol. As you do this, observe the casing being ejected and allow the slide to use its force to shut each time it is pulled to the rear. Refer to Figure 8-9C. You can rotate the slide towards your non-firing hand to assist in working the slide to the rear.

Figure 8-9C

Figure 8-9D

Figure 8-9E

Step Four: Properly insert and seat a loaded magazine with a hard palm. Refer to Figures 8-9D and 8-9E.

Step Five: Rack the slide fully to the rear and release it to close by its own spring tension. Your pistol is now ready to continue the engagement. You can rotate the slide towards your non-firing hand to assist in working the slide to the rear.

Step Six: Continue the engagement as the situation dictates. Refer to Figure 8-9F.

Note: Correcting this malfunction needs to be practiced often since it is the most complicated to do under stress (when you lose dexterity because blood is leaving the extremities to supply the major organs with fresh oxygen). Be sure to lock the slide to the rear FIRST so you will consistently correct this malfunction 100 percent of the time.

Figure 8-9F

CHAPTER NINE

COMBAT MARKSMANSHIP
CONSIDERATIONS, TRAINING TIPS & DRILLS

After you become proficient in the fundamentals of marksmanship, you will progress to combat marksmanship. The main objective of combat marksmanship is the use of the pistol to engage threats at close range with quick and accurate fire. In a gunfight, it is not the first round fired that wins, but the first accurately fired round. You should always use the sights when engaging the threat, the only exception being if this step would place the pistol within arm's reach of the threat.

Tactical Survival Rules

Use your senses: *Your eyes and ears can be of great advantage if used to detect sights and smells that are not normal. Slow down or stop periodically to listen for any noise that is not normal in that environment.*

Never turn your back on any uncleared area: *Systematically clear during your search of an area. This rule applies indoors and outdoors.*

Keep your balance: *Never move faster than you can accurately shoot. Leaping around corners and sliding down hallways is not tactically feasible.*

Stay away from corners: *Use angles to maintain an advantage. Pie off corners and be ready to fight when the situation allows it; maintain some distance to increase your reaction time.*

Use and maximize the distance: *Use distance to your advantage and do not hug a danger area or assailant. The closer you are to a threat, the easier it is for them to hit you or attack you. Trust your ability when it comes to the range to the threat.*

Take the initiative and/or advantage: *At every point in a gunfight, you should be taking advantage of whatever you can to fight and survive. Good losers are dead.*

Do not remain static: *Move when the situation allows it, i.e., move after shooting, during magazine changes and/or malfunction corrections. But be careful not to move and draw attention to yourself if the situation does not allow it.*

Consider your wardrobe: *Watch what you wear, i.e., a light-colored shirt is nice to present a front sight onto. Try for the darker colors, depending on the area of operations.*

Maintain your alertness: *You should not be surprised. If you are searching for an individual, do not be shocked when you finally find him/her; plan what to do and prepare. Situational awareness is paramount to survival and stress management.*

Be confident in your ability: *Be cool, do not act cool. Make yourself believe in your ability to prevail and think that your opponent is not as well trained and prepared as you and will not be able to succeed. Do not be rushed if you can afford it; be calculating and decisive.*

Monitor your commands: *Be aware of the commands you give individuals. If you tell them to raise their hands, you will expect this movement and allow them to get ahead of you if they draw. His calculated action may be quicker than your reflexes; remember, action is faster that reaction!*

Continue your education: *Learn from individuals that have been there and done it. You can learn from their mistakes instead of making them yourself and getting the same result.*

Hand-and-Eye Coordination

"Poorly coordinated shooters may achieve proficiency by being closely coached and critiqued."

Hand-and-eye coordination is very important, but not always a natural, instinctive ability of all shooters. It is usually a learned skill obtained by practicing the use of the flash sight picture. The more a shooter practices raising the pistol to eye level and obtaining a flash sight picture, the more natural the relationship between shooter, sights and target becomes. Eventually, proficiency elevates to a point at which the shooter can accurately engage targets in low-light conditions with little or no use of the sights. Poorly coordinated shooters may achieve proficiency by being closely coached and critiqued. Since pointing the index finger at an object and extending the pistol toward the target are much the same, the combination of the two is natural. Making the shooter aware of this ability and teaching him how to apply it when firing result in success when engaging threat targets in combat situations.

Your choice of weapon, equipment, ammunition and training will greatly affect your ability to progress and become consistent. With this in mind, research what you are training for and acquire the correct equipment. It all must be reliable, not pretty.

The eyes focus instinctively on the center of any object observed. After the object is sighted, the shooter aligns his sights on the center of mass, focuses on the front sight and applies the proper trigger press straight to the rear. Most crippling and killing hits result from maintaining the focus on the center of mass. As you progress, your sight picture will "soften" and not be as clear as you focus between the front sight and the target; this is very fast and accurate when attained. Both eyes must be used so you are not limited as to your field of view, and they will be open during high-stress situations anyhow—train as you fight.

When a shooter points, he instinctively points at the feature on the object on which his eyes are focused. This point explains why shooters shoot the pistol of their threat: they are focused on their threat's pistol when they fire. Objects like badges assist in giving opponents a point to look at and use instinctive shooting to hit more accurately than if they tried to use their sights. An impulse from the brain causes the arm and hand to stop when the finger reaches the proper position. When the eyes are shifted to a new object or feature, the finger, hand and arm also shift to this point. This inherent trait can be used by the shooter to engage targets rapidly and accurately. This instinct is called hand-and-eye coordination.

Flash Sight Picture

Flash sight picture is usually used when engaging a threat at pistol ranges; the shooter has little time to ensure a correct sight picture. The quick kill (or natural point of aim) does not always ensure a first-round hit. A compromise between a correct deliberate sight picture and the quick kill method is known as the flash sight picture. As the shooter raises his pistol to eye level, his point of focus switches from the threat to the front sight, ensuring that the front and rear sight are in proper alignment left and right, but not necessarily up and down. Pressure is applied to the trigger as the front sight is being acquired and the hammer falls

Figure 9-1

as the flash sight picture is confirmed. Initially, this method should be practiced slowly, gaining speed as proficiency increases. Remember that "slow is smooth and smooth is fast." Take your time and perform the techniques correctly and speed will show up.

In pistol-distance shooting situations, time is seldom available to apply precisely all of the fundamentals of marksmanship. When a shooter fires a round at a threat, many times he will not know if he hit his target. What the threat is wearing may not lead to your seeing a response, and you should be looking at your front sight anyhow. You must "call your shot"—that is, know where your front sight was on the target when the weapon begins recoil. Therefore, you must practice using a series of shots to incapacitate the threat, not the old two shots and look. You may choose to practice the double tap engagement (two shots in rapid succession "hammers"); the controlled pair (two well-aimed shots); or a series of shots until the target has ceased being a threat (three to five rounds). I will detail the uses of these engagement methods, and you may make your choice.

Double Tap

Double tap is two shots fired with flash sight pictures at fairly close targets. To perform a double tap, you determine that the distance to the target is close enough for your ability to perform a double tap. This distance will change with your ability level, the size of the target and the amount of practice you have performed recently. The shots are fired as soon as you obtain your acceptable flash sight picture. This technique is learned on a range; you must see how you shoot with different sight pictures and figure out how fast your double taps can be to keep the needed accuracy. A good time to practice for is 1.2–1.4 seconds from position three on a full silhouette-sized target at seven meters. The shots are not meant to be in the same hole or close to each other; it is to create quickly at least two wound channels in separate parts of the threat.

Controlled Pair

Controlled pair is two well-aimed and well-placed shots at moderate pistol ranges. This distance will also come from experimenting with different speeds and different sizes of targets to obtain your acceptable results. The key to the controlled pair is that you see three distinctive sight pictures: one before the first shot, one before the second shot and one after the recoil recovery. This method is the preferred engagement method when you have encountered a need for discriminating shooting, where you must hit only the intended target. These two shots should go exactly where you were aiming.

Shoot Until They Stop

You may also practice neutralizing a threat with the "shoot until they stop" method of engagement. This method can be three to five shots to the center of mass or the failure-to-stop-type drill. In the common failure-to-stop drill, engage the threat with two rounds to the center of mass, then one to the center of the head. Other variations are to fire two rounds to the center of mass then fire two rounds into the hip/pelvic area to break the pelvic girdle in case the threat is wearing body armor. This approach is more valid than the head shot since the hips are larger than the head and not as likely to be moving as much as the head. These types of engagements may be needed to neutralize the threat from a drug-crazed assailant or a very determined, well-trained and well-equipped opponent.

Traversing

In close-shooting situations the threat may be attacking from all sides. The shooter may not have time to change position constantly to adapt to new situations. You should practice traversing from all your shooting positions. Traversing is nothing more than pivoting your upper torso in the direction that is easiest to engage the threat. Some shifting may inevitably occur, but this approach is for extreme situations with survival in mind. If possible, maintain the triangle formed by your two-handed grip with nearly locked elbows to keep your recoil management. By moving your foot, you can quickly pivot to change angles.

Weapon Retention

Weapon retention is used to fight and/or protect yourself from having your weapon taken away and avoiding contact shots. Your non-firing hand is instrumental in blocking or grabbing and pulling an attacker, depending on his actions. Make sure to roll the pistol out (slide out) so it does not hit you when it cycles, which may induce a malfunction. Ensure you do not shoot your non-firing hand with this technique.

Figure 9-2

Contact Shooting

Contact shooting involves placing the pistol against the adversary and shooting. This technique will ensure rounds onto meat, but will also most likely induce a malfunction. As in Figure 9-2, train to keep your pistol back and in a retention position induce a malfunction (the Bullins Factor).

Multiple Threats

You must determine how you are going to handle a multiple-threat situation. There are numerous techniques for this. You must take into account your ability, distance to threats, the size of the threats, actions of the threats, your available cover, and more. I will not advocate any one method as you must decide and live or die by it. You can determine to shoot single shots across the bank of threats and continue back and forth until the threats are neutralized. This technique is based on the idea that multiple wounded threats are at a disadvantage rather than completely stopping one and then working on the next. What works at shooting matches is not always what works for real. Test your theories with Simunitions and you will see how they are really applied. This single-shot technique can be transformed to two shots, three shots, etc., depending on your decision.

Indexing

Regardless of method of engagement, you must learn to index between threats by looking to the center of mass of the next target before you bring your weapon to it. This approach allows you to place your front sight quickly and precisely while not over-swinging past your intended center of mass sight placement. Practice letting the recoil assist you in the movement to the next target. Ensure you have let out just enough slack on the trigger to re-engage the sear and begin the pressure rearward on the trigger so that you may engage the moment your front sight reaches the center of mass.

Rhythm Drill

The rhythm drill is used to develop smooth rhythm, speed, accuracy, proper follow-through and recovery. Beginners should get a shooting timer for accurate records of progress. Firing a string of shots with a rhythm allows the shooter to measure and improve upon a multitude of tasks. A rhythm to practice for is no more that .06 seconds between the split times between shots.

Example: The six-shot rhythm drill is designed to develop/test three separate skills. First is the ability to hit the target, second is the ability to acquire the target in a prescribed time frame, and third is the ability to control the trigger squeeze in a smooth, deliberate rhythm. On a larger scale, this drill identifies the shooter's target acquisition and trigger management abilities and also builds both speed and accuracy.

Professional standards place the adversary at about seven to 10 yards, a composite time of three seconds or less, with no more than .06 seconds between any of the six shots. For example, if the second shot breaks .25 seconds following the first shot, the shot break for each of the following shots must be within .06 seconds of the second shot break. A realistic example follows below:

Shot Number	Shot Time	Split Time 1-2-3-4-5-6
1	1.05	.30
2	1.35	.31
3	1.66	.33
4	1.99	.35
5	2.34	.30
6	2.64	

In this example, the time requirement of three seconds was met and there was a range of only .05 seconds between any individual shot. Assuming that each shot was on target, the standard was met. Conversely, if shot number three had a time of 1.73 seconds with a separation of .38 seconds, it would have exceeded the separation break by .02 second (.38 minus .30 = .08), and the shooter would have failed to meet the standard.

To perform a rhythm drill properly with your desired accuracy, you have to command all of the fundamentals mentioned previously. Further development of these skills will increase speed and accuracy. The breaking of the rhythm or the rounds failing to impact in the desired group size will highlight improper grip, stance, lack of proper trigger control, poor recoil management or improper sight alignment/sight placement. You can make the rhythm drill as many rounds as you would like for practicing the cadence and proper accuracy. Once the rhythm drill is mastered, you can apply it to engaging multiple targets and gradually reduce the amount of time used to complete the drill. A proper rhythm can be more accurate and faster than the standard double tap, double tap, double tap. Get a timer out and try it for yourself.

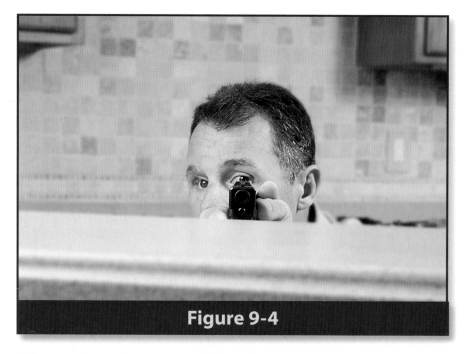

Figure 9-4

Shooting From Behind Cover

There are two ways of shooting from behind cover: over it or around it. The preferred technique is to shoot over it. Shooting over cover offers a wider arc of coverage and provides a more stable base if the cover is used as a platform for the weapon. In addition, it doesn't matter whether the shooter is left-handed or right-handed. Remember to not silhouette yourself against a contrasting background because you will be more easily seen. Be back far enough from the cover to fully present without touching or going past it; economy of effort and economy of motion equals efficiency and speed. Refer to Figure 9-4 do not shootthe cover (the Treschuk Factor). Remember, the bore is lower than the sights, so take this into account and do not shoot the cover. Refer to figures 9-4, 9-5A, and 9-5B.

Shooting Over Cover

(Vehicles or Medium to Low Walls)

The shooter should assume a squatting position behind the cover. For lower cover, you may have to assume a kneeling position so as not to expose yourself. The pistol should be presented and ready to shoot. As the shooter comes up from behind the cover, he should expose only enough of himself to make the shot. When shooting over cover, the shooter may use the cover as a shooting platform, provided the pistol does not extend beyond the cover. When using this technique, the shooter should never rest the pistol directly on a hard cover. The bottom of your hands will be padding between the cover and the pistol.

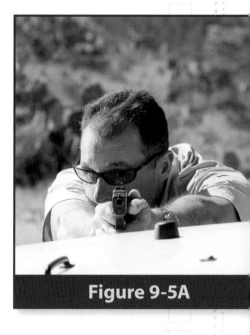

Figure 9-5A

Keep in mind rounds ricochet or travel across hoods of vehicles and walls. In this case, it is better to stay back and give yourself at least two to six feet of distance from the vehicle or walldepending on the angle of return fire suspected.

Figure 9-5B

Figure 9-6A

Figure 9-6B

Shooting Around Cover

(Standing, Sitting, Kneeling and Prone Positions)

As in shooting over cover, the shooter should set up as close to the cover as possible when the pistol is mounted in a firing position. This position will expose less of his body to multiple targets as he comes around the cover. Refer to Figure 9-6B. He should shoot the pistol from the primary side (i.e., right-handed going right or left-handed going left) so as to expose less of the body. Refer to Figures 9-6A and 9-7A.

If the shooter is not experienced in weak-hand shooting, he should employ a lean technique when going to the non-firing side. When standing or kneeling, the shooter takes a short, quick step out, just far enough to engage the farthest outside target, and then arcs inward, engaging targets as they appear. The technique from the prone position is similar, except that instead of stepping out with the foot, the shooter moves his outside elbow and then rolls to complete his arc. Be aware of how much of your body you are exposing around the cover. Try varying your foot placement with different cover situations to minimize exposure.

Weapon Transition

You must change to the secondary (pistol) when your primary weapon fails. Pick one technique that will work for you with the equipment and duties you have. If at all possible and the situation allows, by all means seek correct cover and perform your weapons transitions.

Figure 9-7A

Figure 9-7B

| Figure 9-8A | Figure 9-8B |

Close Quarter Battle (CQB) Sling Method

The use of a close-quarter battle (CQB)-type sling is very common among operators in military and law enforcement SWAT or direct action-oriented missions. The technique of transitioning to the secondary (pistol) weapon from an empty or malfunctioning primary (rifle or shotgun) is simple, as you normally just release the primary. There are variations of this that assist in limiting the movement of the primary as you transition.

One of these techniques is to twist the primary with the non-firing hand as you bring it down; with AR-15/M4 and MP5-type weapons, the magazine and sling create tension to hold the weapon against the body. Remember to practice as you fight, and do not wear shorts when do-

Figure 9-8C

Figure 9-8D

ing transition training as when you sear your leg with a hot barrel, you will learn the hard way. Also, some of the mentioned techniques can cause damage to your weapon's finish; this is up to you, but a scratch will not hurt many work weapons, and one day it may save that second you need to survive. Refer to Figures 9-8A through 9-8E.

Figure 9-8E

Figure 9-9A

Figure 9-9B

Figure 9-9C

Figure 9-9D

| Figure 9-9E | Figure 9-9F |

Traditional Sling Method

Notice that both hands are moving at the same time so as not to waste time and effort in Figures 9-9A through 9-9E. This transition could be used if you are not actively in a fight and need to get your pistol or keep an empty weapon you have more ammunition for and will tactically reload when the situation allows it.

Figure 9-10A

Figure 9-10B

Figure 9-10C

Figure 9-10D

The Drop Down Method

In Figures 9-10A through 9-10D, both hands are also moving at the same time so as not to waste time and effort. Maintain a grip with the non-firing hand on the primary weapon and begin your draw of your pistol. Refer to Figure 9-10B. Let the buttstock drop from the pocket of the shoulder. Refer to Figure 9-10B. The weapon is now hanging straight down, and when the buttstock is approximately thigh/knee high, let the weapon drop onto the butt and fall forward toward the threat. Refer to Figure 9-10C. Slight pressure is needed to ensure it falls forward. This impact can assist in freeing a stuck casing, making it easier to clear a malfunction, if present, when the engagement is over. As you are ridding yourself of your empty or malfunctioning primary weapon you are going to a kneeling position. Refer to Figure 9-10C. This movement may cause your opponent to lose his sight picture or you could be utilizing available cover to protect yourself during the transition. Remember, you are usually either moving or shooting, rarely at the same time; the situation and your abilities dictates. Continue the engagement as needed from the kneeling position if this is tactically feasible.

> *"Your method of engagement and fundamentals should not change."*

Use of a Protective Mask

Shooting with a protective mask or gas mask must be practiced if it is used in your line of work. Your method of engagement and fundamentals should not change. You must have your current prescription optical inserts if you usually wear glasses in your everyday activities. Restricted breathing is the biggest factor to adjust to. And with masks that are not full face, you have a limit on your vision and this limit must be known and practiced with. Physical activity with the mask on will obviously cause condensation inside the mask to form, so you may need to treat your lenses with an anti-fog substance. Placing pieces of paper towel or toilet paper inside the mask will allow for the moisture to be drawn to them rather than the lenses.

COACHING & TRAINING PRACTICES

This section will help teach you methods to practice your shooting efficiently and safely. Treat going to the range like going to the gym; pick a focus and then do just that and go home. Progression is a key, but do not progress faster than you can perform correctly.

Dry firing: *This is the most effective and cost-efficient type of training. All you need is an empty pistol and a safe place to practice. You may choose to use a small piece of ballistic armor material or a ballistic vest in a room if you want to guarantee that a negligent discharge does not exit the room and injure someone.* **Never have loaded magazines or ammunition in the room in which you are dry firing.** *Thoroughly check your pistol and magazines to ensure they do not contain live ammunition. You may choose to purchase dummy ammunition or dummy magazines for dry firing. Begin your practice session like any other, by having the objectives for your practice. Know what you are going to emphasize in each practice session. Apply the proper techniques and take your time. You can never miss fast enough, so begin slowly. Most modern pistols are not affected by moderate dry firing. A coach, if you have one, is also a valuable dry-firing tool to identify what you are doing correctly and incorrectly.*

Figure 9-11

Ball and dummy drill (for live-fire practice): *In this method, a coach loads your pistol or magazines for you. He may hand the shooter the loaded weapon or an empty one. When firing a pistol (with an empty chamber or dud round), the shooter observes that, in anticipation of recoil, he is forcing the weapon downward as the hammer falls. Repeated practice of this drill will alleviate recoil anticipation.*

Calling the shot: *To call the shot is to state where the bullet should strike the target according to the sight picture at the break of the shot, for example, "to the right," "dead center," etc. If the shooter is not calling the shot correctly in range fire, he is not concentrating on the correct sight alignment. Consequently, he does not know what his sight picture is as he fires. You may also use the clock system for calling the shot. Example: "three inches at three o'clock" is three inches directly to the right of center of mass.*

Slow-aimed fire practice: *This exercise is one of the most important for any shooter and is used to evaluate your use and understanding of the fundamentals. This practice is the use of all the shooting fundamentals for each shot fired. Take your time and review the fundamentals before each shot. Do not rush a shot; it is better to start over and do it right than to waste a shot. You should not hold the pistol up at position* four for more than five to seven seconds; if you do, just pull back to position three and then start from there. You can think in your head on what you personally have to concentrate. Some say "front sight, press" until the pistol fires to concentrate on their sight picture and trigger control. Remember that the proper trigger control allows the hammer to fall without the front sight moving. Some movement is acceptable, but practice to minimize it. And remember to call the shot after each shot. To build speed, perform the actions in a technically correct manner and focus on minimizing movements (economy of motion and effort equals speed). You should build speed by sometimes speeding up to miss 30%, then slowing back down to 100% hits, a push/pull method.

Air pistols: You may use air pistols to provide realistic low-cost training. The fundamentals all still apply, just on a different type of pistol. Remember the safety considerations also apply.

Figure 9-12

Timers: The usefulness of an affordable but dependable shooting timer cannot be overstated. Used properly, it will give you a true figure to calculate your progress. The basic timer can track your time of shots and the split time between shots. Refer to Figure 9-12.

Shooting chart for the right-handed shooter

(Left-handed shooters use a mirror image to diagnose)

 Breaking wrist down.
Not concentrating on the front sight (front sight low).
Anticipating recoil and jerking trigger.

 Applying too much or too little finger to trigger.
Improper placement of pistol in hand.

 Applying strong thumb pressure.
Anticipating recoil (pulling the trigger at angle).

 Jerking the trigger (snatching).
Canting the weapon to the left and allowing the barrel to drop.

 Squeezing the whole hand with the trigger squeeze.
Slack wrist.
Jerking the trigger.

 No specific error; all prerequisites for a clean shot are lacking.
Lack of front sight focus.

 Not leveling the front sight in rear sight.
Unsteady weapons platform.

 Not centering the front sight in the rear sight notch.
Unsteady weapons platform or unequal grip pressure.

Pulling back on the weapon when firing.
Breaking of the wrist (heeling).
Not concentrating on the sight alignment
(front sight too high/looking over the top of the rear sight).

SHOOTING DRILLS FOR PRACTICE

(Presented in the order of progression)

1. Dry Firing Practice: *The use of dummy cartridges, dummy weapons and/or dummy magazines to practice new techniques or for warm-up exercises.*

2. Ball-and-Dummy Drill: *The practice technique of loading a dummy round into the chamber or within a loaded magazine by the coach so the shooter will see if they are performing proper fundamentals. If shooter anticipates the blast or recoil, they will pull the pistol and interrupt sight placement.*

3. Slow-aimed Fire: *Fundamental marksmanship practice to utilize all the fundamentals and have the bullet go where desired by the shooter.*

4. Presentation Position Three to Four Drill: *This drill is essential to learn to break the shot at the point of full extension and hit your desired target. This drill must be mastered to progress in speed or accuracy with whatever type of automatic pistol you use.*

5. Controlled Pairs: *The practice of attaining two well-aimed and well-placed shots from the holster or position three to build confidence or practice shots of distance and/or small targets.*

6. Double Taps: *Practicing to attain the rapid secession of shots and maintain your desired accuracy. Emphasize proper focus on the sights and minimal movement of the trigger.*

7. Drawing From a Holster: *The proper four-step draw sequence is one of the foundations for further progress. This techniques must be learned correctly and remain consistent for further progress.*

8. Rhythm Drill: *This drill is to practice trigger control and recoil management and leads to speeding up on multiple targets by smoothing out a cadence of shots. They must be a set of shots at a steady rhythm, depending on the designated target or targets.*

9. Kneeling Drill: *Practicing how you will kneel for various situations and practicing with the equipment used.*

10. Prone Drill: *Practicing how you will use the prone position for various situations and practicing with the equipment to be used.*

11. Supine Drill: *Practicing how you will use the supine position for various situations and practicing with the equipment used. Remember where your feet are!*

12. High Barricade: *A drill utilizing a high horizontal barricade to let you practice setting up your standing position and shooting over it or around it.*

13. Low Barricade: *A drill utilizing a low horizontal barricade to let you practice setting up your position and shooting over it from the prone, sitting and/or kneeling positions around it.*

14. Turning Left/right Drill: *These drills are designed to allow you to practice how much movement is needed and the specifics of getting to the oblique to make the shot.*

15. Turning About Drill: *This drill is designed to allow you to practice how much movement is needed and the specifics of getting to the rear to make the shot. Also called the P.R.A. drill—perceiving a threat, recognition of a threat, and acquiring the threat with the pistol.*

16. Weapon Retention: *This drill is designed to allow you to become more familiar and comfortable firing from position two of the draw.*

17. Move Forward, Stop, Shoot Whistle Drill: *This drill is used to get you shooting at someone else's command, forcing you to be comfortable in shooting during movement.*

18. Move Forward and Shoot Whistle Drill: *This drill is used to get you shooting at someone else's command, forcing you to be comfortable in shooting during movement.*

19. Strong-hand Draw Drill: *This drill is used to build your confidence in shooting with only your strong-hand when your non-firing arm is injured or unusable.*

20. Weak-hand Draw Drill: *This drill is used to build your confidence in shooting with only your non-firing (weak) hand when your dominant firing arm is injured or unusable.*

21. Shooting From A Vehicle: *This drill is used to familiarize the shooter with shooting out of a vehicle effectively. You can always get a new windshield, but not a new life.*

22. Shooting Into A Vehicle: *This drill familiarizes the shooter with how to shoot effectively a threat in a vehicle.*

23. Shooting While Wounded, Strong-hand Reload: *This drill is used to build your confidence in reloading with only your strong hand when you non-firing arm is injured or unusable.*

24. Shooting While Wounded, Weak-hand Reload: *This drill is used to build your confidence in reloading with only your weak hand when your firing (dominant) arm is injured or unusable.*

25. Shooting While Wounded, Strong-hand Malfunctions: *This drill is used to build your confidence in correcting malfunctions with only your strong hand when you non-firing arm is injured or unusable.*

26. Shooting While Wounded, Weak-hand Malfunctions: *This drill is used to build your confidence in correcting malfunctions with only your non-dominant (weak) hand when your firing arm is injured or unusable.*

Important Notes

- Keep finger off the trigger until on target and ready to engage.

- Maintain control—know where your pistol is pointed at all times.

- Only go as fast as your ability allows and attain a 100 percent hit standard for the combat mindset when your life depends upon it.

- Slow is smooth and smooth is fast. Get faster by eliminating excess actions/movements, not just by speeding up.

- Remember to shoot correctly and not to shoot excessive amounts. For me, 350 rounds a day is the maximum for a good training day.

- Push yourself to missing up to 30 percent, then slow back to 100 percent hits into your acceptable target size—improve speed and accuracy.

- Treat range practice like going to the gym— plan your session, keep records, use coaches (that know what they are talking about) and leave when the results are attained—focus on what you are wanting to improve.

- Finish range sessions with a drill you do well to build/maintain confidence.

- Consistent, proper procedures and proper training will build confidence, speed and accuracy.

CHAPTER TEN

SHOOTING WHILE WOUNDED

The most advanced pistolcraft is conducting shooting-while-wounded drills with both the strong and weak sides. These techniques will save your life when the chips are down. The key is to never quit the fight. If you have to head butt the aggressor to death, then this is what you will have to do. Your adrenaline will allow you to do amazing acts in the worst situations, so use it to save your life or others' lives.

NOTE: These techniques are dangerous if practiced incorrectly, so be very aware of the details. If you doubt your ability to conduct these drills, seek professional instruction so you may learn them safely.

You should practice as if you have been wounded *before* you could draw your pistol and *after* you have drawn your pistol, with both your strong and weak hands. Holster selection and placement come into play, as some body types are more advantageous than others. You will still have to tailor these techniques so they work for you, but remember to watch your muzzle direction and keep the finger off the trigger when not on target and willing to engage.

Both kneeling and standing positions are detailed. Kneeling is preferred if tactically feasible due to the low center of gravity; you are a smaller target and close to the ground if you drop something.

Strong-hand Shooting While Wounded - Standing

I will begin explaining shooting while wounded with the non-firing hand being wounded from some form of injury, whether from gunshots or a car accident. Think about how your non-firing hand is most likely to be wounded as your attacker is shooting center of mass, and if you are at full presentation, this is where your arms are. This technique is one of the simplest since you are used to drawing with just your strong-hand, but your presentation from position three to position four is different. I will begin with standing while shooting with the strong hand and progress into magazine changes and malfunction correction drills.

Step One: As you draw your pistol with your strong hand, bring your wounded arm to the centerline of your chest as best you can (Figure 10-1). This position helps with balance and recoil management.

Step Two: As you present your pistol towards the threat, step your firing foot towards the threat and present a side profile to your threat. This step will allow the recoil to come through your arm to your upper torso, and you will be better able to handle the pistol while shooting. Lean slightly forward from the hips.

Step Three: At full presentation, slightly cant your pistol to the left (no more than 45 degrees) to allow you to tighten your wrist and use the larger muscles of your forearm to force the recoil through your arm to your torso (Figure 10-1). Align the sights and press the trigger straight to the rear.

Figure 10-1

Figure 10-2A

Figure 10-2B

Strong-hand Shooting While Wounded, Magazine Change

Kneeling

Step One: Go to a one-knee "kneeling position"kneeling position. As you go down, you can depress the magazine release to drop the magazine or place the pistol behind your knee that is up. (Figure 10-2A through 10-2D). While pinching the pistol behind your knee, if not pre-

Figure 10-2C

Figure 10-2D

viously removed depress the magazine release and remove the used magazine. Drop that magazine and locate the fresh magazine in your magazine pouch by reaching across your body to your magazine pouch (Figure 10-2E).

Figure 10-2E

Step Two: Properly insert and seat the fresh magazine with the palm of your hand (Figure 10-3B). Only glance at your magazine well as you begin to put the magazine in it; then refocus on the threat (Figure 10-3C).

Figure 10-3A

Figure 10-3B

Figure 10-3C

Figure 10-4A

Figure 10-4B

Step Three: Regrip the pistol (Figure 10-4A). If the slide is locked to the rear, you only have to release the slide with the slide release using your thumb (Figure 10-4B). If the pistol's slide is closed, use the technique of cycling the slide by hooking the rear sight on your boot, belt, holster, or whatever is available (Figure 10-4C and 10-4D). Once the rear sight is hooked, force the pistol down and away to cycle the action and ensure that clothing or equipment doesn't interfere.

NOTE: Ensure your finger is off the trigger during any malfunction or magazine change actions or the pistol will fire once cycled.

Figure 10-4C

Figure 10-4D

Step Four: Continue the engagement as the situation dictates (Figure 10-5). Remember to slightly cant the pistol to the left to tighten up your arm to allow for greater recoil management or straight up as normally fired.

Figure 10-5

Figure 10-6A

Standing

Step One: Whether you are changing your magazine because it is empty or you want to recharge the pistol with a fresh one in the standing position, remember to seek protective cover, not just concealment. If reloading due to a slide lock by an empty magazine, (Figure 10-6A). Depress the magazine release button prior to holstering the pistol (Figure 10-6B). Insert the pistol into your holster and remove the magazine and put it in a pocket if performing a tactical reload to top off the pistol (Figure 10-6C.)

Figure 10-6B

Figure 10-6C

Figure 10-7A

Step Two: With the strong arm, remove a fresh magazine from your magazine pouch and insert it into the magazine well. Utilize the proper grip on the magazine as described earlier, index finger extended on the front of the magazine and pinched by the thumb and middle finger (Figure 10-7A). You may have to glance quickly at the magazine well to ensure the magazine goes in the first time attempted (Figure 10-7B). Once the magazine is in the magazine well, shift your focus back to the threat area and firmly seat the magazine to ensure it is locked (Figure 10-7C).

Figure 10-7B

Figure 10-7C

Figure 10-8A

Figure 10-8B

Figure 10-8C

Step Three: Regrip your pistol and draw it from the holster (Figure 10-8A). If the slide is forward, you will use whatever you have on you or near you to rack the slide to the rear to cycle the next round. You can use your belt, holster, corner of a wall or door, or a pocket (Figure 10-8C). If the slide is already locked back, you only have to press down the slide release with the strong-hand thumb.

Step Four: Continue to fight (Figure 10-9).

Figure 10-9

Figure 10-10A

Figure 10-10B

Strong-hand Shooting While Wounded - Malfunctions

Correcting malfunctions should be conducted from the two-knee kneeling position if tactically feasible. This lowering of the body helps with balance when you are under great stress and allows you to easily pick up anything from the ground if dropped accidentally. It is very important to seek bulletproof cover while correcting malfunctions with one hand. The practice of these malfunction drills is essential to correct the malfunction safely when you have the disadvantage of using just one arm. The symptoms of the malfunction are the same as previously covered for each type of malfunction.

NOTE: All actions with the pistol except the actual shooting are performed with the finger off the trigger; this point is very important to prevent negligent discharges while operating.

Failure to Fire - Kneeling

Slide is forward on an empty chamber or the pistol was loaded with a dud round. The correction is the same as with two hands, except you are using just the good arm.

Step One: Once you have detected a failure to fire, immediately remove your finger from the trigger guard. **SLAP** the butt of the pistol on your thigh to seat the magazine positively (Figure 10-10B).

Figure 10-11A

Figure 10-11B

Figure 10-12

Step Two: RACK the slide to the rear and allow it to shut by its own spring tension. You can also force the slide to the rear by hooking the front sight of the pistol on your belt, holster, boot or pocket (Figure 10-11A and 10-11B). Be very aware of your muzzle direction and ensure that your finger is off the trigger. Since this is a critical act, you may have to shift focus to ensure your slide is correctly placed. Immediately regain focus toward the threat once the sight is placed correctly.

Step Three: READY, continue the engagement as the situation dictates (Figure 10-12).

Failure to Fire - Standing

Slide is forward on an empty chamber or the pistol was loaded with a dud round. The correction is the same as with two hands, except you are using just the good am.

Step One: Once you drop the hammer on an empty chamber or on a dud round, immediately remove your finger from the trigger and the trigger guard. SLAP the magazine into the magazine well by firmly seating the butt of the pistol on your thigh (Figure 10-13B).

Figure 10-13A

Figure 10-13B

Figure 10-14A

Step Two: RACK the slide to the rear by hooking your rear sight on your belt, holster, pocket or whatever you have available. Since this is a critical act, you may have to shift focus to ensure your slide is correctly placed (Figure 10-14A and 10-14B). Immediately regain focus toward the threat once the sight is placed correctly.

Step Three: READY, continue the engagement as the situation dictates (Figure 10-15).

Figure 10-14B

Figure 10-15

Figure 10-16A

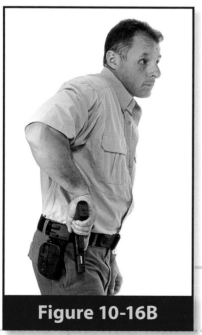

Figure 10-16B

Figure 10-16C

Failure to Eject

The empty casing is not fully ejected and is pinched in the slide. This corrective action is as simple as with two hands. Standing and kneeling may be done in the same way.

Step One: Once you have identified that you have a stovepipe malfunction, immediately remove your finger from the trigger guard. Using some part of your belt kit or boot, rest the protruding casing against it and vigorously push against the casing and force it to be released by the slide (Figures 10-16A through 10-16C). Ensure you do not fully work the slide to the rear as this may induce a double feed malfunction.

Step Two: Continue the engagement as the situation dictates. Refer to Figure 10-17.

Figure 10-17

Figure 10-18

Failure to Extract

The spent casing is not extracted from the chamber, and the next loaded round is being forced in behind it. Standing or kneeling uses essentially the same correction.

Step One: Once you have identified a double-feed malfunction, immediately remove your finger from within the trigger guard. Refer to Figure 10-18. Lock the slide to the rear by moving the pistol in your hand so you can engage the slide release with your thumb. While pushing up on the slide release with your thumb, hook the rear sight on your belt kit or boot and force the slide to the rear (Figure 10-19). You may have to shift

Figure 10-19

your focus to ensure you lock the slide to the rear quickly.

Step Two: Remove the magazine by pushing the magazine release button with your thumb (Figure 10-20) and work the action at least three times to ensure the stuck casing has been ejected (Figure 10-21A and 10-21B). Use to hook your rear sight onto your boot or belt to cycle the pistol.

Figure 10-20

Figure 10-21A

Figure 10-21B

Figure 10-22A

Figure 10-22B

Figure 10-22C

Step Three: Place the pistol into your holster muzzle down between your knees, remove a fresh magazine (if not previously done), and then properly insert and seat the fresh magazine (Figures 10-22A through 10-22C). Since this is a critical act, you may have to shift focus to ensure your magazine is inserted into the magazine well correctly. Immediately regain focus toward the threat once the magazine is started into the magazine well. Remove your pistol from your holster once the magazine is locked in the magazine well.

Figure 10-23A

Figure 10-23B

Step Four: Cycle a round into the chamber by once again hooking the rear sight on your boot, belt or whatever you have that will do it, and force the slide to the rear and allow it to return by its own spring tension (Figure 10-23A and 10-23B).

Step Five: Continue the engagement (Figure 10-24). Remember to cant the pistol no more than 45 degrees to the left to use the stronger muscles in your forearm to tame the recoil or straight up as normally fired.

Figure 10-24

Figure 10-25A

Weak-hand Shooting While Wounded

Weak-hand shooting while wounded is the most difficult technique for most to learn. Careful study and proper practice will help you perfect this valuable training. The first problem you will encounter while shooting with your non-firing hand is getting to your pistol, which is on your strong side. Below are some different techniques you may study to see what works for you and your body style.

The Draw

You may be able to draw your pistol by pulling your gunbelt around to your non-firing side so you can reach your pistol (Figures 10-25A through 10-25C).

Figure 10-25B

Figure 10-25C

Figure 10-26A

Figure 10-26B

Figure 10-26C

Figure 10-26D

You may be able to reach around your front to turn the pistol in your holster and get the proper grip and draw the pistol (Figures 10-26A through 10-26D).

Figure 10-27

You may have to pull your gunbelt toward your non-firing side to assist you in drawing your pistol with your non-firing hand (Figure 10-27).

Magazine Change - Kneeling

Step One: Once you have decided to perform a non-firing hand magazine change, pinch it between your thigh and calf muscle (Figure 10-28A and 10-28B). Depress the magazine release and remove the magazine.

Figure 10-28A

Figure 10-28B

Figure 10-29A

Figure 10-29B

Step Two: Remove a fresh magazine from your magazine pouch, properly insert it into the magazine well and firmly seat it with the heel of your hand (Figures 10-29A through 10-29C).

Figure 10-29C

Figure 10-30

Step Three: If the slide is locked to the rear, simply shut it by pushing down with your index finger on the slide release to allow it to shut (Figure 10-30). If it is closed, you must rack the slide (keeping your finger off the trigger and outside the trigger guard) using your belt, boot or whatever is available (Figure 10-31A and 10-31B).

Step Four: Continue the engagement as the situation dictates (Figure 10-32).

Figure 10-31A

Figure 10-31B

Figure 10-32

Figure 10-33

Magazine Change - Standing

Step One: Once you have decided to perform a non-firing hand reload while standing, you need to seek protective cover. Release the magazine by pushing on the magazine release with your non-firing hand index finger (Figure 10-33). If the magazine does not fall out of the magazine well, you will have to strip it with your pocket or your gunbelt (Figure 10-34A and 10-34B)).

Figure 10-34A

Figure 10-34B

Step Two: Either pinch the pistol between your knees or replace it in the holster backwards and insert the fresh magazine from your magazine pouch. Be sure to seat the magazine firmly to ensure it is locked in place (Figures 10-35).

Step Three: Now you must load the chamber by shutting the slide if it is locked to the rear, and this step is done by pushing down on the slide release with your non-firing hand's index finger. If the slide is shut you must rack the slide with your belt, pant pocket or whatever you have available (Figure 10-36).

Step Four: Continue the engagement as the situation dictates (Figure 10-37).

Figure 10-35

Figure 10-36

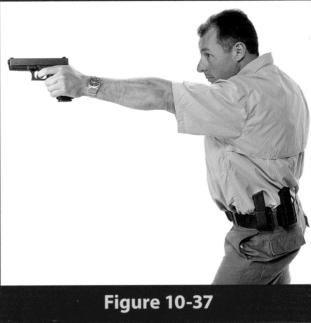

Figure 10-37

![Figure 10-38](photo of man in shooting stance)

Figure 10-38

Weak-hand Shooting While Wounded - Malfunctions

Failure to Fire

Both standing and kneeling are very similar (Figures 10-38 through 10-40). SLAP, RACK, READY.

Figure 10-39

Figure 10-40

Failure to Eject

The corrective action for the stovepipe-type malfunction is the same as for the strong-hand technique, but it is performed with the non-firing hand. Sweep the stovepiped casing out of the action.

Failure to Extract

The spent casing is not extracted from the chamber, and the next loaded round is being forced in behind it. Standing or kneeling uses essentially the same correction. Employ the strong-hand technique, except you must practice locking the slide to the rear by pushing up the slide release with the trigger finger. Refer to strong-hand Figures 10-18 through 10-24.

Step One: Once you have identified a double-feed malfunction, immediately remove your finger from within the trigger guard. Lock the slide to the rear by moving the pistol in your hand so you can engage the slide release with your trigger finger. While pushing up on the slide release with your trigger finger, hook the rear sight on your belt kit or boot and force the slide to the rear.

Step Two: Remove the magazine by pushing the magazine release button with your trigger finger and work the action at least three times to ensure the stuck casing has been ejected. Hook your rear sight onto your boot or belt to cycle the pistol.

Step Three: Place the pistol muzzle down between your knees or in your pants pocket, remove a fresh magazine and properly insert and seat the fresh magazine.

Step Four: Cycle a round into the chamber by once again hooking the rear sight on your boot, belt or whatever you have that will do it and force the slide to the rear and allow it to return by its own spring tension.

Step Five: Continue the engagement. Remember to cant the pistol no more than 45 degrees to the left to use the stronger muscles in your forearm to tame the recoil.

Picking Up Your Fallen Pistol

During a gunfight where you have sustained injuries to one or both of your arms, you will probably need to pick up your pistol to continue the fight. This action sounds simple, but stress makes the simplest tasks more difficult. These techniques are meant to allow you to train as you fight, so you should practice these as detailed below.

If the butt of the pistol is facing your firing side, you must simply lift up the slide with the non-firing hand as you begin to form your strong-hand grip and roll the pistol into your hand (Figures 10-41A and 10-41B). If the butt is facing your non-firing side, simply roll the butt across so it is facing the other way and do as described above. Consistency will build confidence, speed and accuracy.

Figure 10-41A

Figure 10-41B

Picking up a pistol with only your firing hand when the grip is facing your firing side (Figure 10-42) and away from your non-firing side (Figure 10-43). Use your thumb to help hold the pistol in your grip until you have lifted it from the ground.

Figure 10-42

Figure 10-43

Figure 10-44A

Figure 10-44B

Picking up with your non-firing hand when the grip is away from your firing side (Figure 10-44).

Step One: Reach across the pistol so you can lift up the butt of it (Figure 10-44A).

Step Two: As you roll it over to your non-firing side, begin to form your one-handed grip (Figure 10-44B).

Step Three: Once you have fully rolled the pistol over and you have your correct one-handed grip, you can continue the engagement (Figure 10-45).

Figure 10-45

CHAPTER ELEVEN

LOW-LIGHT SHOOTING

The use of white lights to aid your shooting in low-light situations is not to be understated. This section is not called night shooting, since in a basement at noon it may be just as dark as at midnight; these situations are low light. You can encounter many situations where a white visible light source—a flashlight—can greatly increase your chance of survival.

The advantages are that white light sources are available to all, inexpensive and easily maintained. You need not buy the biggest and best light, but you must buy a dependable one and have it with you when you need it.

Check out www.bhigear.com for quality lights and accessories. White lights offer the quickest means of identifying targets and searching areas. The shooter uses his pistol sights just as he does in daylight situations. Be aware that the light can compromise your location if you are using it near an undetected threat. Also, it may be accidentally activated and give away your position at an inappropriate time.

You must decide what type of light you are going to use and decide when you are going to use it. Many companies are now adding a flashlight pouch on their magazine pouches as the importance of such items is now being rediscovered. I will discuss the different shooting techniques with flashlights, and you may tailor them to the flashlight and technique you like. You may also decide about the light types that mount onto your pistol. This light is by far the most useful in low-light shooting situations. Quality counts for the pistol-mounted lights, since they must stay securely mounted and the bulb must withstand the repeated recoil or firing.

Tritium sights are available in many types and prices. They are good for low-light shooting when your situation allows you to identify your threat and not compromise your location by using a white light. The most common sight configuration is the three tritium dots; various colors are also available. Remember, when you are deciding which sight to purchase, you get what you pay for. Gunsmith installation may be necessary on some pistols.

Figure 11-1

Figure 11-2

Figure 11-3

Figure 11-4

Low-light Techniques

Various methods you can use:

- **Crossed wrist technique (Also known as the Harries Technique):** Hold the flashlight in the non-firing hand. Cross the hand with the flashlight under the firing hand at the wrist and control the light on/off switch with a finger or thumb of the non-firing hand (Figure 11-4).

Figure 11-5

- **Weapon-mounted light:** Some weapons are designed to have lights mounted on them (Figure 11-5). These are most preferred for precise tactical shooting and general use, and since you use your normal grip it is accurate and quick. Many are now available that quickly attach and detach, which allows the pistols with accessory rails such as the Glock with a Streamlight M6 tactical light (Figure 11-1 and 11-3).

Figure 11-6A

Figure 11-6B

- **Flashlight on the primary weapon technique:** This technique is used when the primary weapon (rifle or shotgun) has a light source mounted on it. If the weapon malfunctions, the light source can still be used. Simply support the weapon with the non-firing arm (Figures 11-6A and 11-6B). Aim the light source/primary weapon at the target and fire the secondary weapon (pistol) using the single-hand firing technique.

Low-light Considerations-

Light Usage During Malfunctions And Reloads

Most operators carry a multitude of lights to serve different purposes. If you can only carry one, make sure it works with all your potential activities. Using handheld lights during malfunction corrections and reloads has to be practiced as you only have two hands. The most common method is to place the flashlight under your firing-side armpit. This placement allows you to use your empty non-firing hand to correct the malfunction and/or reload the pistol. Obviously, if you do not need the light on to correct the malfunction or reload, have it off so you do not give away your location. Once your pistol is ready, you can continue with your situation as you decided.

Light Usage While Shooting While Wounded

If anything can get more complicated, it would be shooting with a light not attached to your weapon while you are wounded. This should help you decide to get some type of weapon-mounted light as you will have the rest of your life (though it may be short?) to work with the flashlight and pistol into a winning combination.

Remember that if you are working with others in a situation where white lights are used, you do not all have to turn your lights on. Use only the amount of light needed to accomplish the given task.

Always plan to have extra batteries and bulbs for replacing when needed to keep the light operational.

Lights can be used to disorient or blind potential threats temporarily when they are first encountered, or as a control technique.

When shooting with a light in low-light, you will notice that your shot groups will be tighter. You have fewer distractions and the sights are silhouetted on the target from the light.

Focus your beam if you have an adjustable head on your flashlight. Too wide a beam can sometimes prevent you from seeing details as clearly as possible.

To search rooms, you can aim the center of the beam at the baseboard/floor or the wall/ceiling; this will maximize the illuminated area.

When searching, use short, sweeping scans and, once you have a quick look, turn off the light and move your position before continuing. Remember, you lose your night vision as soon as you flash, and it takes time to readjust to the level of ambient light. One technique to use is to close your dominant eye to save its night vision; situation dictates. If you must shoot, you can quickly open your dominant eye and engage the threat.

You can practice with a partner to use a "volley fire" (one uses his/her light, then turns it off, and the other uses his/hers) method of searching to confuse and yet still effectively search. You can also just use one light so the other operator is not compromising his position.

Have your weapon ready when you do turn your light on so you can deal with what you see as soon as possible. You should not be surprised to find what you are actually looking for; mentally prepare for the discovery of what you are searching for so you can quickly accomplish the mission.

Remember that the brightness of your pistol's muzzle flash and those of others that are nearby will be affected by the environmental factors, the barrel length and types and amount of powder used. Test and familiarize yourself and your team with the weapons you use so you are not surprised by these effects.

Darkness can be concealment, but is definitely not cover.

You will sacrifice your element of surprise with white light and might want to test and evaluate an infrared (IR) light option utilizing night vision goggles and IR flashlights. Also, you may utilize an IR light beam as an aiming point designator.

Know the moans and groans of your pistol so you can feel malfunctions in low light, as you most likely will not *see* the malfunction. Learn the symptoms of the different malfunctions, their feels and sounds, to know when to conduct the proper malfunction corrective action. As mentioned previously, you can place the flashlight under your firing-side armpit. You may plan a code word with your partners to communicate to them that you are out of the fight with a malfunction. Obviously, seek cover if available and the situation allows it. Once the problem is identified, turn off your light and fix it.

Darkness can be concealment but is definitely not cover, so plan accordingly. Low-light environments only complicate operations, so practice these methods often to become more comfortable and competent at operating in this situation.

CHAPTER TWELVE

LEFT-HAND-DOMINANT SHOOTER

Few references exist for the specific training of left-hand-dominant shooters. Tom Bullins of Trigger Time Valley, a left-handed firearms instructor and shooter, has compiled this chapter for your education. This information will also help right-hand-dominant shooters with their weak-hand shooting.

Very few firearms instructors correctly teach left-handed shooting. Most left-handed shooters are taught to shoot right-handed in the armed forces; also note that most holsters for militaries are right-handed. When Tom was in the Marine Corps, he was charged with protecting some of the nation's most important assets and was forced to use a right-hand holster and a 1911A1 with no ambidextrous safety. He had to put a lot of thought and practice into drawing and firing with this configuration. He noted during training courses that right-handed instructors fail to teach left-handed shooters the correct way to work their pistols.

Considerations since most pistols are made with right-handed shooters in mind:

- The magazine release and the slide release are on the wrong side.

- The decock lever is usually not in an easily reached location.

- The magazine release button may be depressed if you are using an inside-the-pants holster for concealed carry.

- The safety can accidently be disengaged when carrying the weapon in right-handed holsters.

- Adding extensions to magazine releases and slide releases should be avoided; certain extended slide stops do work well on Glocks.

- Utilizing the "slingshot" method to release the slide is a good idea for left-handed shooters when properly done. Maintain the muzzle to threat and pivot the pistol on its bore to the non-firing hand to slingshot the slide. The advantage to the left-handed shooter is that he will not have to regrip the pistol with the firing hand, thus saving time reacquiring the grip and target.

- The magazine release can be depressed by using the trigger finger, and using the trigger finger also may actuate some slide releases.

Cross-eye-dominant shooter considerations—when the shooter is left-handed, but right-eye dominant:

- Move the pistol under your dominant eye or make a small movement of the head to the pistol; make sure the dominant eye is behind the sights of the pistol. This will speed up sight acquisition and increase accuracy.

- Some shooters may have to shut their non-dominant eye to get the correct sight alignment and sight placement.

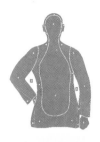

APPENDIX

PROGRESS WORKSHEETS

This Appendix was added for you to track your progress with certain drills, allowing you to focus more on what you have to practice and less on skills you perform well. Be honest with your results so you can have a truthful assessment of your ability and progress. You can determine the number of rounds and type of targets on some of these charts or re-designate them for your needs.

ONE-SHOT DRAW

Date	Distance	Time

SPEED RELOAD

Date	Distance	Time

PRESENTATION FROM POSITION 3 TO 4

Date	Distance	Time

DOUBLE TAP

Date	Distance	Time

180-DEGREE PIVOT

Date	Distance	Time

FAILURE-TO-EJECT MALFUNCTION

Date	Distance	Time

SHOOTER'S CHOICE _____

Date	Distance	Time
_____	_____	_____
_____	_____	_____
_____	_____	_____
_____	_____	_____
_____	_____	_____
_____	_____	_____

SIX-SHOT RHYTHM DRILL

Date / Distance		Shot Time	Split Times
_____	1	_____	_____
_____	2	_____	_____
_____	3	_____	_____
_____	4	_____	_____
_____	5	_____	_____
_____	6	_____	_____
_____	1	_____	_____
_____	2	_____	_____
_____	3	_____	_____
_____	4	_____	_____
_____	5	_____	_____
_____	6	_____	_____